FEATURING ESSAYS BY

Veronica Chambers

Luvvie Ajayi

Lena Waithe

Brittney Cooper

Kid Fury

Ylonda Gault

Maria Brito

Melissa Harris-Perry and Mankaprr Conteh

Meredith Broussard, with visualizations
by Andrew Harvard and Juan Carlos Mora

Elodie Mailliet Storm

Michael Eric Dyson

Reshma Saujani

Candice Benbow

Carmen Perez

Isabel González Whitaker

Edward Enninful

Fatima Robinson

Ebro Darden

Treva B. Lindsey

Robin M. Boylorn

Caroline Clarke

QUEEN BEY

QUEEN BEY

A CELEBRATION OF THE POWER AND CREATIVITY OF BEYONCÉ KNOWLES-CARTER

EDITED BY

VERONICA CHAMBERS

ST. MARTIN'S PRESS ★ NEW YORK

www.stmartins.com

Brittney Cooper's essay first appeared in Cosmopolitan.com.

"Beychella Is Proof That Beyonce Is the Greatest Performer Alive. I'm Not Arguing." Copyright © 2019 by Luvvie Ajayi.

Quotation from "The beginning" from *Brown Girl Dreaming* © 2014 by Jacqueline Woodson. Used by Permission of the Author.

Designed by Anna Gorovoy

Library of Congress Cataloging-in-Publication Data

Names: Chambers, Veronica.
Title: Queen Bey : a celebration of the power and creativity of Beyoncé
    Knowles-Carter / edited by Veronica Chambers.
Description: First edition. | New York : St. Martin's Press, 2019. | Includes
    bibliographical references.
Identifiers: LCCN 2018050716 | ISBN 9781250200525 (hardcover) |
    ISBN 9781250240491 (International, sold outside the U.S., subject to rights
    availability) | 9781250200532 (ebook)
Subjects: LCSH: Beyoncé, 1981—Criticism and interpretation.
Classification: LCC ML420.K675 Q4 2019 | DDC 782.42164092 [B]—dc23
LC record available at https://lccn.loc.gov/2018050716

Our books may be purchased in bulk for promotional, educational, or business use. Please contact your local bookseller or the Macmillan Corporate and Premium Sales Department at 1-800-221-7945, extension 5442, or by e-mail at MacmillanSpecialMarkets@macmillan.com.

First U.S. Edition: March 2019
First International Edition: March 2019

10 9 8 7 6 5 4 3 2 1

For Liba Daniels-Halisi Bagley and Cassandra O. Butcher—
Sister friends, Dance floor Divas, Goddesses, Queens

Contents

———•———

CONTENTS

CONTENTS

QUEEN BEY

Introduction:

What Might a Black Girl

Be in This World?

———•———

VERONICA CHAMBERS

I first became aware of Beyoncé in the late nineties. I was a young editor at *Newsweek* magazine, where my purview included writing about music. My apartment in Brooklyn Heights was like my own version of the Barbie Dream House: top floor of a brownstone, super high ceilings, two levels to the apartment— living room and kitchen on the first floor, loft bedroom and alcove on the second floor. All of my friends from L.A. had keys to my place. My friend John Singleton wrote a draft of his remake of *Shaft* on my couch. A decade plus before companies like eBay and Rent the Dress, my friend Cassandra—who lived in California—and I FedEx-ed dresses back and forth for big events. I went to and hosted some truly epic parties.

It was a golden age for women in contemporary R&B. I would make playlists with all my favorites: Mariah Carey's "Breakdown" with Krayzie Bone and Wish Bone from Bone Thugs-N-Harmony. Aaliyah's "Are You That Somebody?" Every track from Missy Elliott, every track from Erykah Badu's womynist debut. Deborah Cox's "Nobody's Supposed to Be Here." Vanessa Williams' "Colors of the Wind." Toni Braxton singing anything and everything. Destiny's Child, especially that early Wyclef Jean remix—because Lauryn Hill was the queen of hip hop in those days—were easy to slip into the mix.

"Independent Women" by Destiny's Child was a game changer. The 2001 song was the theme song to a remake of *Charlie's Angels* starring Drew Barrymore, Cameron Diaz, and Lucy Liu. Destiny's Child had been through some personnel changes. There had been, rumors had it, more than a little drama behind the scenes. But by 2001, there was no denying that Destiny's Child—reassembled as a trio with Beyoncé clearly as the lead—was pure fire. Beyoncé at the head of a boardroom table in the "Independent Women" video was everything I—and every young woman I knew—wanted to be: glamorous, in charge, with her best girls by her side. Beyoncé 1.0 had arrived, and the way she held the camera's gaze made us feel as if hers was a party we were all invited to.

A side note. While I recognize the role that colorism has played in the African American community as well as in mainstream culture, I find it to be a retro and useless conversation.

Why give so much air time to a phenomenon so many of us agree shouldn't exist? But because it comes up again and again in reference to Beyoncé, let me say this: I would argue that Bey's most defining characteristic isn't her skin color or the length or texture of her hair. What makes Beyoncé so undeniably Beyoncé is the fire in her belly, the almost otherworldly level of focus and ambition in her eyes.

Growing up as an Afro-Latina in America, in a country marked by constant reminders of race and racism, I have been asking and answering one question my whole life: what might a Black girl be in this world? The incredible body of work that comprises the oeuvre of Beyoncé Knowles-Carter seems to me an answer to that question too. What might a Black girl be in this world? Everything—and more than you ever imagined.

Dozens of movies came out the year that "Independent Women" dropped and Beyoncé began to truly captivate our imagination, but hardly any of those films featured brown-skinned girls. I enjoyed *Legally Blonde* and *Tomb Raider,* but I didn't see anyone who looked like me in those films. *Amélie* and *Gosford Park* remain perennial favorites, but no depiction of diverse women in those films either. *Ocean's 11* and *Charlie's Angels* were great romps but as an audience member, they didn't feel like romps that Black and brown girls were invited to. So "Independent Women" became, if you will, a trailer—a promise, before the term was even widely used, of all the Black girl magic that was to come. When the history of Black women in the twenty-first century is written, Beyoncé's place, her work as a marker and reflection of power and possibility, will be undisputable. She is more than a pop star. Her very omnipresence means she sits, again and again, at the intersection of intersectionality.

In 2002, I married the love of my life. It had been—to my mind—a whirlwind romance. He proposed after seven months of dating. We got married a year later. Three months after we married, I was invited to teach in Maine at Bowdoin College. My husband stayed behind at our apartment in New York. But three out of four weekends, he flew up to visit me. I would drive from my little riverside cottage in a small town called Woolwich and pick him up at the airport in Portland. What might a Black girl be in this world? Anything and more than she imagined.

Growing up on Ocean Avenue in Brooklyn, I never imagined myself in Maine—quiet afternoons sitting by the Atlantic Ocean, exchanging my recycling for a handful of wrinkled one dollar bills, enough money to buy fresh lobsters from fishermen at the wharf. I'd never imagined, growing up in Brooklyn in the '80s listening to Héctor Lavoe and Run DMC that I'd be on a head nod hello basis with craggy New England fishermen. I didn't ever picture myself on a leafy campus, a newlywed, a published author. My life had changed so fast. But no matter how quickly things changed, Beyoncé's music always kept up with me, a soundtrack of power and possibility.

On Friday nights, when I went to pick my new husband up at the airport, I hopped in my old Volvo and I would play the first track to feature Beyoncé as a solo artist: "'03 Bonnie and Clyde." I loved that song, more than I loved some relatives of mine. I still do. I'd play it on repeat, the windows rolled down, the smell of pine and fir trees mixed with the smell of salt air. Even when I couldn't see the ocean, I could smell it. I loved that about Maine. It took me about an hour to drive to the airport. Sometimes I played the song five times on repeat. The love that B and Jay shared was a mirror to my own newlywed love. And then there was a sweet bonus—the song included a sample of Tupac's "Me and My Girlfriend."

I'd known Tupac and his mother, Afeni. My first book was a behind-the-scenes look at John Singleton's sophomore film, *Poetic Justice.* I spent six months on the set from casting to wrap and I discovered that movie sets are like greenhouses, forcing into bloom friendships that might otherwise take years to cement. I never claimed to be a pal of Tupac, but every time I would see him afterward, he would beeline and hold me tight. The refrain of "All I need in this life . . . / is me and my girlfriend" felt like a hug from my new/old friend, as if Tupac were rolling with me through the woods in Maine.

It became clear in the 2000s that Beyoncé's one-name moniker was hard earned, well earned. Beyoncé was as synonymous with music as Sting or Prince, Michael or Bono.

The moment that captured my attention was in 2010, when she hit pause on everything. Her mother had advised her that maybe a break was in order and she heeded that advice, taking nearly a year off to "live life, to be inspired by things again." She visited, and sometimes revisited, all of the places she never really got to see when she was on tour: museums and ballet performances, Glastonbury—as a fan not a performer—the Great Wall of China, and Australia. In an article in *Essence,* she wrote:

Visiting a country without an itinerary was so appealing to me. After a few days in Auckland, New Zealand, for the start of my husband's tour, I settled in Australia for five weeks . . . I had no schedule while taking in the sites of Melbourne, Brisbane, Perth and my favorite Aussie city, Sydney. They have the best restaurants and the harbor is awesome. It was a carefree existence for me . . . In London I met Sade, one of my favorite artists. I've loved and admired her for so long. In Russia I found vintage jewelry and saw the ballet *Swan Lake*. But what is being abroad without enjoying the food? All over Italy the streets smell like gelato. In Paris my nephew Julez and I had escargot for lunch and it was actually tasty (though not as good as a funnel cake at the Houston Rodeo). In Capri I ate pizza and drank red wine every Sunday . . . I'm drawn to the ocean. Whether it's jumping from a yacht (those photos drive my mother crazy; she thinks it's dangerous), swimming, snorkeling in the Red Sea (I've never seen fish so breathtaking), or just walking on the sand, the sea has a calming effect on me. Croatia has the most beautiful water—although it's the saltiest I ever tasted. I floated on my back for close to an hour in the Mediterranean Sea. It was one of the best moments of my life.

It was a wow moment for me, the moment when Beyoncé became synonymous with another word—power. Even at the highest levels of entertainment, there seems to be this constant unrelenting, one might even say merciless, pressure to keep producing, to stay in the game, lest you slip even an inch in the pop culture pantheon. Beyoncé's break was mega to me, because it was as if she was declaring, "I have no doubt or concern about staying on top." She was playing her own game. She was writing her own rules. While it would be awhile before she declared herself Queen Bey (and, occasionally, King Bey), I think the hiatus she took in 2010 was her first truly sovereign act. She would later sing in her song "Pretty Hurts" that she was trying to take the crown without falling down. But the break, the time she took away from the spotlight, signaled that at 30, she had quietly and confidently ascended to royalty. She was no longer just another pop princess. She was a queen in the industry of her choosing and she would wear the crown for life.

The writers in this anthology take you through the rich discography and visual, creative universe of Beyoncé's work. They explore the "mic drop" years when she surprised and wowed us with music that we never saw coming. They explore all the ways in which she laid her personal pain bare and invited us to be human alongside her, to rage, to grieve, to rebuild and reassemble, and always to celebrate the joy of just being alive. The brilliant Brittney Cooper, who declared that Beyoncé is her feminist icon, writes about why Jay-Z's apology on *4:44* matters so much to all women, but Black women in particular. Ylonda Gault writes about sisterhood, betrayal, and the kind of trouble that might ensue when you have a "billion dollars on an elevator." Luvvie Ajayi talks about how the force of Beyoncé's cultural influence and love of culture spans from HBCUs (historically Black colleges and universities) to Afro-Futurism and the wonder that was Beychella.

British *Vogue* editor Edward Enninful discusses her style because oh, yeah, she's the best dancer and an amazing singer, she art directs, and she's a mogul, but she's also a fashion icon. I love how Emmy award–winning writer/actor/producer Lena Waithe gives us a personal take on growing up in Generation Beyoncé and how YouTube star Kid Fury recounts learning Bey dance routines in his childhood bedroom and explains what Beyoncé means to the gay community. Apple Music DJ and legendary New York music executive Ebro. Darden discusses how Bey changed the music business for everyone. Famed dancer/choreographer Fatima Robinson, known for her jaw-dropping work with artists such as Pharrell and Kendrick Lamar, talks about the way Beyoncé moves and how contemporary dance and hip hop culture grew up together.

Isabel González Whitaker writes about the power of Beyoncé singing in Spanish and how the Venn diagram of where Southern culture and Latinx culture connect is bigger than we sometimes think: It doesn't get more Latin than loyalty to lip gloss and a mother's ire at stepping out of the house undone. "When you look at beauty and the Southern black girl it can be indistinguishable from beauty as presented in Dominican culture or Cuban culture," says Africana Studies expert Zandria Robinson. "There's a shared focus on beauty, elegance, femininity and the presentation of the self."

Award-winning data journalist Meredith Broussard explores how Beyoncé's work has shaped the current landscape of popular culture, and Elodie Mailliet Storm unpacks all the clues and truths in the very private star's very revealing Instagram account. Acclaimed art advisor Maria Brito writes about Bey's fine art obsessions and how her curated portraits draw on influences that range from Botticelli's *Birth of Venus* to the Mexican patron saint, Our Lady of Guadalupe, from Klimt to Andy Warhol to contemporary Afro-Futurist artists.

Caroline Clarke writes about the power of watching her daughter grow up in the Beyhive. Robin Boylorn, a professor at the University of Alabama and a member of the Crunk Feminist Collective, explores Beyoncé's Southern roots while Treva B. Lindsey checks the rhyme on the artist's hip hop influences and how she fits (surprisingly well) into the pantheon of female rappers.

Reshma Saujani writes about how Beyoncé inspires her to stay connected with her own cultural identity, and Carmen Perez, one of the co-founders of the Women's March, details just how revolutionary Beyoncé's musical activism can be.

Michael Eric Dyson writes a heartfelt, powerful analysis of how Beyoncé and Michael Jackson connect creatively and why he believes she has surpassed the King of Pop.

Not every author in this book is a superfan. Melissa Harris-Perry and her former student Mankaprr Conteh tussle about their differing takes on Beyoncé: addressing everything from colorism to class politics. And there's much more.

As I'm writing this, Bey and Jay have just released their video for "Apesh*t," which was shot in the Louvre. The Louvre video hit home because France in general and Paris, in particular, has been part of my narrative for a long time. My maternal great-grandmother, Flora, was from Martinique. I was born in Panama, raised in Brooklyn, and grew up speaking Spanish and English. Flora, who helped raise me, spoke French. In college,

I dreamed of spending a year abroad in Paris. But my financial aid package wouldn't cover the study abroad programs. At 25, I took my first trip to Paris. At 35, I'd worked and saved and managed to give myself—and my husband—a very late, but truly Black girl magical, junior year abroad. What might a Black girl be in this world? Everything. And where she might go? Everywhere.

Beyoncé Giselle Knowles has worked so hard, for so long, that she deserves a serious, thoughtful exploration of her life and her work. She's still so young. When this book publishes, she'll have just turned 37. And yet her career trajectory has more than 25 years of runway. It occurred to me that it makes sense that we were watching Bey dance, pose, and sing her way through the Louvre as we put the finishing touches on this book. This collection of essays is almost like a museum retrospective of the solar system that is Beyoncé. Here we have the early works. Here, we have the fashion wing. This section explore love and marriage. In this corridor, the writers look at Bey as performance artist. In this room, the writers explore how motherhood has influenced and shaped her work. In this room, the writers explore the erotic in her work.

Again and again, Beyoncé has reminded us that she has no interest in separating herself from the struggle of being a Black woman in this world. On the contrary, that struggle is a bass line in her music, one that reverberates in her pride in being one of us, the highs and the lows of our collective inventiveness and creativity. As she stated in the September 2018 issue of *Vogue*, "I come from a lineage of broken male-female relationships, abuse of power, and mistrust. Only when I saw that clearly was I able to resolve those conflicts in my own relationship. Connecting to the past and knowing our history makes us both bruised and beautiful." Just let those last few words sink in for a second, "bruised and beautiful."

The poet June Jordan once wrote, "Like a lot of Black women, I have always had to invent the power my freedom requires." Those of us in the Beyhive acknowledge Beyoncé as a goddess (and certainly, celestial clockwork is a theme that resonates for her, as she sings in "Apesh*t": "Call my girls and put 'em all on a spaceship"). But this book reminds us that hers is a uniquely American story about a girl, born in Texas, who shaped a vision of womanhood that has influenced men and women of every generation all around the world. It's about a young woman who steadily and assuredly invented the power her freedom required. What might a Black girl be in this world? She might become queen of all she surveys.

All hail Queen Bey.

Beychella Is Proof That Beyoncé Is the Greatest Performer Alive. I'm Not Arguing.

———◆———

LUVVIE AJAYI

Beyoncé Giselle of House Knowles. First of her name. Snatcher of Edges. Killer of Stages. Citizen of Creole Wonderland. Legendary Black Girl. Queen.

I gotta up my intake of Biotin and re-order my supply of Jamaican Black Castor Oil. Beyoncé stays coming for all my new growth. I'm not even mad cuz I'd gladly sacrifice some coiffure for the Queen.

I didn't go to Coachella, but I was a citizen of Beychella, watching her performance and realizing more and more that we were watching a legend. That is not an overstatement. If

Beyoncé decides she's sick of us lessers and never releases another piece of music, she has already earned icon status and I'm not here to argue with you. People have been crowned icons for doing and being less.

But this woman, who has made history over and over again, and did it again by being the first Black woman to headline Coachella, took the chance to cement her place as the greatest entertainer alive.

LET ME REPEAT: Beyoncé is the greatest performer alive. And if you disagree, there's hateration where your heart used to be. This should be undisputed. Tell me who else has the showmanship, the excellence, the choreography, the voice. If you can't, stay out of the fray. People have been saying Janet Jackson. Listen here. I LOVE ME some *Damita Jo*, just like the next, but this ain't the era of "Rhythm Nation." She is forever GREAT but she is not at her prime (which is okay because she's also 20 years older than Bey). I said what I said. Stay nauseous.

The reason why I'm especially staking this claim is that Beyoncé does it while making a point to be as BLACK AS POSSIBLE. There is something really special about watching Bey in all her NOIR PIXIE DUST, reminding folks over and over again that Blackness is something to be proud of.

She sang the Black national anthem, while a 100-person all-Black band was behind her giving all the life. They did a full stepshow, while wearing branded sweatshirts in the tradition of historically Black Greek letter fraternities and sororities. They even stepped as she told people to "suck on her balls." Then she changed into a costume with a crest on her chest. The crest had the eye of Horus on it and four segments: Queen Nefertiti,

14

a Black Panther, a fist up, and a bee (for the Beyhive). She played Malcolm X's "Black woman" speech. She paid tribute to Fela Kuti.

For two hours, she performed for a mostly white Coachella audience, with very few white faces on that stage. But really, she performed for the millions of Black people she knew were tuned in online everywhere. It was a brilliant display of excellence. It was a performance of bravado. It was a musical that I'd watch on Broadway over and over again.

I think back to when *Lemonade* dropped, and how it was an ode to diasporic Blackness. The fact that she is so committed to paying some serious homage to her Blackness, and her Africanness, and the diaspora just makes my spirit hit the shoki and azonto. Plus, she does it on such grand stages so she makes sure the world consumes her pride. *Lemonade* had Bey rocking some braids with baby hair, to prepare people for all that Nubian. She had women in all types of hairdos sprinkled through the film. There are righteous afros, luscious weaves and braids, standing around looking like an army of ancestral blessings. But what stood out so prominently in that Black-ass video was Bey's homage to Afro-spiritualism. From her "Sorry" song up, she featured elements of Ifa religion (hey Oshun in that yellow dress), with dancers, the face painting, and even a water ritual. In the words of Yoruba people, "awon omo egbe" showed up. Her connection to that divine was as Black as she could get. She talked about generational curses, and breaking them. She gave glory to the Orishas throughout this video. SO AFRICAN. I almost wanted her to serve up jollof rice.

This woman then got on one of the biggest concert stages

in the world and re-affirmed her pledge to Onyx Magic. I coulda lost my good mind in glee.

That ain't even touching the fact that she then brought out Mr. Knowles-Carter. And then Destiny's Child reunited. And then Solange came out to dance for her life with her sister. It was stunning. It was a feast for the senses. As your eyes were dancing along with Bey and her crew, your ears were overwhelmed because she also sounded her best.

We were watching a living legend at her best. Six months after birthing twins. She never looked winded. She danced and sang for two whole hours at top energy. She is a marvel. I've never had kids and I did a karaoke routine of Sister Act 2's "Joyful, Joyful." Four minutes where I was two-stepping and lip syncing. I got off the stage and had to sit down for ten minutes to catch my breath.

And that is why I have spent a lot of today arguing with people online. I feel like this performance took me to the point of no return in my fandom. I've always been a Beyoncé fan. I buy all the albums. I know ALL the songs. I even write about how I lose my shit about her work every time she comes out. Read: my "Formation" blog post. But I hadn't been a member of the Beyhive. I hadn't been dragging folks on her behalf. That has changed. I just sent in my membership dues. I'll bring Flaming Hots to the next meeting.

HOW CAN ANYONE DENY THIS WOMAN'S TALENT?!?! People have definitely tried it today and my patience is out. How can you watch what she does and still be like "meh?" At this point, it's foolishness.

Here's the thing. I'm not saying people need to declare

Beyoncé queen of their hearts. But the woman is EXCEL-LENT. The levels people go to, to criticize her excellence, are mind-boggling. When you spent hours, every day, practicing your craft, for 25 years. And you show up and give everything you have. And you honor your culture. And you show up for people who look like you, yet people can still be all "MEH." Or people say "she can't sing" even though you are belting out songs a cappella on key at octaves you don't speak at. It begs the question: at what point can people do and be enough? It's also a lesson for everyone: NO MATTER HOW GOOD YOU ARE, THERE WILL BE PEOPLE WHO DON'T LIKE YOU. And that is okay. Keep doing what you were doing anyway. There are people who don't think Beyoncé is talented. So you KNOW there will be people who don't think your work is remotely good. Keep doing it anyway.

All I know is that Beychella has inspired the fuck outta me. This woman is on top but still shows up as if every performance is her first and last. She acts like she still NEEDS to impress people (like it's her first time), and leaves everything she has on the stage as if it's the last time we'll see her. She's constantly trying to do herself because she's not in a race with anybody but who she was yesterday. She doesn't take being at the top for granted, and that makes me appreciate her artistry and her personhood and her work ethic like nothing else. I will revel in her greatness, and I will side-eye anyone who dares try to diminish what she's done.

YES. I AM OFFICIALLY AVAILABLE TO DRAG PEO-PLE WHO DISAGREE.

She makes me so proud to be a Black girl. And I am

emboldened to be able to say a Black woman is the best entertainer alive.

P.S. Sooo . . . my Beyhive membership kit. Can it come with pins? I need to rock it on my jackets. I also need my T-shirt in a size extra-schmedium, please.

On the Journey Together

---•---

LENA WAITHE

I was in junior high when Destiny's Child released their first video: "No, No, No." I remember me and my friends, all the Black girls, seeing this different kind of Black girl, one we hadn't really seen before. They all seemed like us but there was also something very Diana Ross–ish about Beyoncé, even at the very beginning, where your eyes were drawn to her. You didn't even really understand why, but you knew it wasn't just about the vocals. I gravitated to all of them so easily and so quickly, and I remember thinking, "They're like me. They're like us." I could see something of me in them, in her. They were our generation.

Beyoncé was also a Black queen. I saw in her Diana Ross but also Lena Horne and thought: *So that's what beauty is. That's what it means to be hot. That's what it means to step in the forefront.*

I also immediately wanted to protect her, like she was my bud. Years after I first saw her perform with Michelle and Kelly at the House of Blues in Chicago, when she stepped out for her first solo album, I remember thinking, *Oh man, I hope this is good.* I was nervous for her because I loved Destiny's Child, every iteration of it, and didn't want any of their success or power to go away. Of course, it didn't, it grew.

In a way we're all on the same journey with Beyoncé. I remember seeing her be so confident and also coming into her own womanhood. I moved to L.A. in my twenties, where I was trying to find my own confidence and my own womanhood. That's when I was really listening to her music and relating to her journey in terms of exploring who I was as a woman, as a person, as a Black woman. And now, especially where I am in my career and looking at her, I understand that idea of having to go through a baptism where you bless yourself with the water and you ordain yourself a new woman. Only then can you step forward.

I appreciate also that she knows the journey is never crystal clear. It's not always smooth. It's not always a direct path. Sometimes there are things that you do that you regret. Sometimes you take a step back and then you take a step forward. As I've gone through the challenges in my life I've been looking at the challenges of her life, and she gives you permission to stumble a little bit but then make something beautiful out of that stumble. She proves you can survive like a phoenix no matter what the world throws at you.

I fell in love with my fiancé when the self-titled *Beyoncé* album hit. I wanted the things she talked about in that album, to feel that passion and connection to someone.

Lemonade is the album that lifts us up, all of us. With *Lemonade*, she talks about surviving heartbreak and betrayal. There's just something so human about it and so brave. It's also the album that represents community, where she included all these women that she admires, like Serena Williams. She showed how she survived that time of her life as a Black woman, finding people in her circle to look to when she was struggling and looking for someone to say, *Okay, that person is strong so I can be strong.* When you hear the song "Sorry" for the first time, you're blown away by Warsan Shire's poetry. She's putting people in the public eye you ordinarily wouldn't know about or care about. But because Beyoncé is uttering this person's words, this brown woman's words, we all go out and look for her and find her. Beyoncé used *Lemonade* to shine a light not just on herself but on a community of women of color, to tell their stories and to share their journeys. And she may not have won a Grammy for best album for *Lemonade,* but that won't make people listen to it any less. If I hadn't won an Emmy for the Thanksgiving episode of *Master of None*, that wouldn't make people feel any less connected to it. Black women have always been the backbone of everything. Black women have never sat back.

Beyoncé shows that we're all made of the same stuff; we are all in the same boat. She makes it her business to say, *I'm a mother, a wife, I'm an activist, I'm a daughter, I'm a friend.* We're all friends in this life even if we're different. And no matter how big or small your voice is, she reminds us that we have to stand tall because our ancestors did. So who are we not to do it as well? It doesn't matter who you are or where you come from or what your means are. Look at how she holds up her love for Houston. I'm from Chicago and both cities have their issues, but we know there is beauty in these cities that other people may look down on. But to attach Beyoncé to Houston makes people hold the city and that community in a special place versus saying, *Oh that city over there.* To speak to our cities is to remind people there that you can stand where I stand.

For gay people, Beyoncé represents a light at the end of the tunnel. She may not be gay, but like Cher and Madonna she's a gay ally and icon in the community because she knows what it means to not be like everybody else and to be unafraid of that truth. There are people all over the world—gay, straight, trans, Black, white—that she speaks to because she can cross all barriers. In that way she's descended from Whitney Houston and Michael Jackson. They were proud African Americans who continued to speak to Black audiences, but they couldn't help but bleed over to other audiences because there was something so pure and special about them. Plus there's the specificity of Beyoncé's work—her music and her heart—that's propelled her. As a writer who writes about my life, I know firsthand it's specificity that brings you a broader audience. The more specific you are, the more willing you are to bare your soul, the more audiences endear themselves to you, feel like they know you and cheer for you. That's when things shift in your career. She's done that multiple times.

I grew up on Whitney and Michael and Prince. We may have lost them, but Beyoncé is not afraid to take on the baton of their talent, of their impact. I remember watching *Being Bobby Brown* and Whitney was in the car and they started talking about Beyoncé. Whitney in a way was giving her stamp of approval. She was kind of saying, *Beyoncé can take it from here.* Whenever I look at Beyoncé I'm always reminded of that. Whitney gave her a touch, a sign to go ahead, a touch that said, *You got it from here.*

Jay-Z's Apology to Beyoncé Isn't Just Celebrity Gossip— It's a Political Act

BRITTNEY COOPER

Many critics have focused on *4:44*'s capitalist message, but for Black women, Jay-Z's personal confessions are deeply significant.

Black men of the hip hop generation are having their *Lemonade* moment with the release of *4:44*. By "*Lemonade* moment," I'm referring to the cultural reckoning that Beyoncé made possible with the April 2016 release of her hit album *Lemonade*. On the album, Bey opened up about her struggles with her husband Jay-Z's infidelity, her father's infidelity to her mother, and how impossible it is to try to convince a man who's treating you wrong to love you right. On 4:44's epony-mous track, Jay apologizes to Beyoncé and all the women he's hurt because of his immaturity. No stranger to heartbreak at the hands of Black men, I, for one, found the apology to be a breath of fresh air. Black men's apologies to Black women matter.

Relationships are hard. Black relationships are harder. This is not because Black people are more broken or more patho-logical than any other group. We are not. But we grow up in a world that says we are. Shaped by racism and its multigen-erational assault on Black families, Black people often have had steep mountains to climb to find our way to each other. Think about how hard it is to find love and make a relationship work when you don't have the added pressure of trying to be a representative of your race or trying not to perpetuate racial stereotypes of your people as romantically unstable, promiscu-ous, and prone to broken families. There is also the trauma of dealing with housing, food, job insecurity, and neighborhood violence that plagues many Black folks.

Since the late 1970s, hip hop music and culture have been primary places where Generation X and millennial Black people have worked out their relational expectations and anx-ieties about how men and women are supposed to act in ro-mantic relationships. For instance, one of Jay-Z's earliest hits, "Can I Get A . . . ," plays out Black intimate anxiety over money. The entirety of the chorus and the back-and-forth between him and female emcee Amil on this track is a battle where the men dismiss women who want them for their money and the women dismiss men who don't have any. All of these expectations about proper performances of femininity and masculinity—about men as providers and women as recipients of that provision—are deeply shaped not only by the lingering effects of racism, but by the sexism that pervades American culture. At the same time that hip hop gave Black men a voice about the ways that they struggle to participate in the patriarchal fantasy mentioned above, it also perpetuated the worst versions of toxic masculinity, styling Black men as emotionally unavailable, violent, hypersexed, immature, and inflexible. Jay-Z's songs "Big Pimpin'" and "Girls, Girls, Girls" are only two tracks from his voluminous catalogue that make these themes clear.

On *4:44*, Jay-Z takes off the mask of Black male impenetrability by taking full responsibility for the near-dissolution of his marriage to Beyoncé, the greatest cultural icon of this generation. Like any good apology, he fully owns his shit. There is no passive passing of the buck. The continual refrain on the song "4:44" is "I apologize." In a follow-up mini-documentary called *Footnotes to 4:44*, he assembles an all-star cast of Black men including Will Smith, Chris Rock, Anthony Anderson, Kendrick Lamar, Omari Hardwick, and others to talk about Black male vulnerability. In it, Jay-Z confesses to building a relationship with Beyoncé that was like a "big mansion with cracks in it." To stay together, they had to tear down this metaphoric mansion and rebuild all over again. Jay says that this process of tearing down and rebuilding is the hardest thing he's ever done, even more difficult than enduring the violence of being shot at during his infamous days as a drug dealer in Brooklyn.

In the aftermath of the album's release, there have been a profusion of thinkpieces from Black men *and* women grappling with the implications of Jay-Z's confessions. I've noticed Black men have focused primarily on the economic principles that Jay-Z raps about, while Black women have more often focused on the meaning of his confession and the way his mistreatment of Beyoncé mirrors Black women's more general struggles with Black men. For instance, the venerable hip hop journalist Greg Tate argues that while the conversation about relationships was important, Jay's focus on collective Black economics and property ownership was of more salience. "Contrary to social-media punting," Tate writes, "*4:44* isn't defined by The Apology—though don't get it twisted: It is one helluva apology, eloquently worded and full of excruciatingly personal detail. But last time we checked there's only one person on the planet who has to find Hov credible in actual life, and as savvy as the scenes-from-a-marriage gambit proved to ensure a boffo opening week, the true focus of this terse and finely composed, fiercely quotable album lies more in politics than romance."

And these politics are a continuation of hip hop's long romance with Black economic nationalism. Since the late nineteenth century, Black thinkers like Booker T. Washington have argued that economic power is the key to Black freedom. Jay-Z seems to buy into this idea, particularly on the track "Legacy," where he says, "generational wealth—that's the key. My parents ain't have shit, so that shift started with me."

But surely Tate knows that Jay-Z has cared about money so much, partly, because he wants to be able to impress women. This is true of most straight men in capitalist America. On

"Can I Get A . . ." Jay asks, "If I wasn't a eight-figure nigga by the name of Jigga, would you come around me, or would you clown me?" Now that Jigga is worth nearly ten figures, he feels the security to ask other questions and to question his own obsession with conspicuous consumption. What does the American obsession with getting money do to the quality of the relationships we value most? The album is nothing if not a grappling with these questions too, and more specifically this truth, which I'll use the poetry of the Bible to make plain: "what does it profit a man to gain the whole world but lose his soul?"

So while I think Tate's take on Jay's economic philosophy is important, the piece also bears a troubling kind of misdirection away from the deliberately intimate and confessional aspects of the album. I have seen many Black male colleagues and friends parrot this line of thinking in the many, many social media conversations that I have had since the album's release. Perhaps it's easier to debate the merits of how Jay thinks about money than to deal with the murkier territory of feelings and culpability for relational failures. But Jay uses his mother, his wife, and his daughter Blue as a kind of moral compass that helps him to remember what the purpose of the money, and the "legacy," should and will be. And since the recent arrival of the newest Knowles-Carter children, the twins Sir Carter and Rumi, these questions of legacy are even more pressing.

Some Black men say simply that what Jay-Z is doing by apologizing is not new and that he doesn't go far enough. These men find his apology rather late and not particularly impressive. To be fair, Black men apologizing in popular culture is not new at all. R&B and the blues would not exist as genres of music without the plaintiveness of Black male regret. In the twenty-first century alone, OutKast's "Ms. Jackson," Usher Raymond's entire 2004 album *Confessions*, every single thing that Trey Songz writes, and rappers like Nas and Drake have dealt with regrets and missteps in relationships.

But none of these men is married to Beyoncé, the veritable baddest chick in the game. And none of these men has been called out nearly so publicly, by their own spouse no less, as Bey called out Jay last year. Let's also not forget the nasty elevator incident in early 2014, when Solange was caught on camera assaulting her brother-in-law in an elevator. The Knowles-Carters are the First Couple of hip hop, and only slightly less important to Black folks under 35 than the Obamas. They've long had some explaining to do. Jay-Z apologizes for the Solange incident too, confirming rumors that Solange was defending her big sister's honor. (Of course, that's no excuse for violence.)

Beyoncé named the pain of a whole generation of Black women who have had to love Black men injured and traumatized by the ravages of Reaganomics, the prison industrial complex, and the war on drugs. Those social assaults on Black life have intimate consequences. They change the otherwise loving nature of the men who come home to lie next to you in bed at night. But for the last couple of decades, Black women have been pathologized as the cause of these problems. We have been called loud, difficult, and emasculating. We have been blamed for the challenges of finding loving relationships with Black men. We have been victims of a wholesale kind of cultural gaslighting. That means we have been called crazy and delusional for pointing out Black men's mistreatment of us.

When Jay-Z admitted that he did everything Beyoncé said he did, he affirmed that she was neither crazy nor delusional. His confession matters. His owning it matters. Anyone who has ever loved someone who has the tendency to provoke them or hurt their feelings, and then deny doing it, knows that that shit is crazy-making. When people apologize for the harm they've caused, they affirm your truth and they take responsibility.

Black women have shouldered so much of the weight and the responsibility for the challenges that Black folks face in relationships. And we have endured 40 years of angry Black men in hip hop telling us that it is all our fault. Jay-Z provides an important corrective to this narrative, and he opens the door for a different kind of cultural conversation to ensue. That cultural conversation invites Black male vulnerability, compassion, and empathy. And this conversation is not just important because of what Black men owe to Black women. Hip hop owes it to Black men to allow them to be more complex and complicated characters than the caricatures of toughness and insensitivity that they often become in popular culture.

Before he became fully woke, Jay once told Harry Belafonte, who had called him out for failure to be more political, that "his presence was charity." Thank the goddess that he has dialed back some of the hubris. His presence is not charity, and his apology has done us no favors, but his vulnerability and courage are a gift. I hope we all figure out how to use it wisely.

All Her Single Ladies

———◆———

KID FURY

*W*hen *Beyoncé's "Single* Ladies" video came out, I was a teenager in Miami. I had experienced tons of bullying—people calling me gay slurs before I realized what they were or even what it meant to be gay—so I spent a lot of time in a bubble at home. I would hide out in my bedroom with the door closed, and my mother would always say, "It's like you're not here anyway, because we don't ever see you. You're always in your room."

In my bedroom, I was more than likely watching the "Single Ladies" video. The first time I saw it I immediately started practicing the dance moves. Because when I saw it, I thought: *I know that the girls are being the gays.* The gays do these dances all the time anyway, so they're going to do this one, too. So then I thought, *There's no way that I'm going to go to a club or a party now and not know this dance.* I watched the video a million times.

My room was really small. I didn't have that much standing or wiggle room. There was a big bed and a whole ton of furniture that belonged to my grandmother because it was her room before it was mine. So there wasn't really enough room to dance, but I made it work even if I fell over a couple of times. By the time I went to my next gay party, I knew every step. When "Single Ladies" came on, as I expected it would, I tore it up and got so many compliments. The girls said that I was the best dancer.

To me, Beyoncé—the biggest performing artist, someone I admired for my entire adolescence—was saying, *I see you all and I love this. This is so dope and I'm going to make a whole entire video of it. No cuts. No anything. It's going to be just us celebrating these dance moves.* I remember when she first released a little clip of her learning the dance, and I thought, *You know what? I don't care what anybody else thinks about me being gay. Beyoncé loves it. And I'm going to go back to the club with my gay ass and I'm going to celebrate.* I felt embraced. With as little as I understood about myself and my experience as a young gay man, it made me feel like I mattered.

I don't know how many artists know or admit this, but when nobody else will have your back it's the gay community that stands with you. There are a lot of people right now that are performing and touring thanks to their gay fans. There are some artists right now waiting for Pride to come around so they'll get booked. We are the ones that will support you even when everybody else stops caring. Obviously that's not Beyoncé, but it matters to me that artists like her acknowledge our community and what we do for them.

When the "Single Ladies" video came out, gay Black and Latino men were J-setting in clubs and at parties. That is basically the style of dance Beyoncé was doing in the video. More recently at Coachella, there was J-setting going on in the bleachers behind her. That strengthens my connection to her; because until she did it, I had only seen gay men doing that kind of dance.

In the "Get Me Bodied" video she had gay dancers and she said "snap for the kids." There were two gay backup dancers in her "Freakum Dress" video too; they got her dressed and beat her face. She made sure to include us to say *I see you all, I hear you all, I love you all, I appreciate you all.* For the biggest performing artist in the world to be using your phrases and your dance moves and your dancers is a way of saying you provide something worthy of recognition in the world of art and performance. It's a big embrace.

I lived in Miami with my Jamaican immigrant parents for the first 25 years of my life. I was very small for most of my childhood. I don't know if it had anything to do with my height, but I had a big mouth; I talked all of the time. I was always trying to tell a joke or do something silly or be the class clown. A lot of the time that would get in the way of me progressing academically. My teachers would always tell my parents, "He's so smart, he's very intelligent. He just doesn't do the work. He wants to talk all the time."

When "Bills, Bills, Bills" came out I distinctly remember being in my grandmother's family room with my cousins, Crystal and Janelle, and I remember the hair salon scene with the girls talking about how awful guys were and they weren't deserving of anything. It was immediately relatable to me—I felt it in my spirit. I knew then that this was who I wanted to be—Beyoncé.

By the time I left high school I had discovered Crunk & Disorderly and Concrete Loop and other Black blogs that were fascinating and with entertaining points of view. I decided to start one myself. I named it Fury and it was just me reporting on pop culture and crazy things that were going on in everybody's backyard and being cynical and cheeky. Eventually that evolved into me starting my own YouTube channel where I would talk about celebrities.

I can't remember the first time I talked about Beyoncé on my channel, but the longest video I did on her was after a concert in Atlantic City. It was my first time seeing her live and obviously it was life changing. I went straight back to my hotel to tape and talked about everything that was so amazing about her. That episode got a great response and ever since I make a video about her whenever she drops an album or a new video. I speak genuinely from my heart about how amazing and otherworldly I think she is.

As a kid I really loved Janet Jackson. I really loved TLC. But Beyoncé was something else; there was something so Southern and Black about her. It was also the cute little outfits that her mama was making for her and the group. She was young and hip and cool and put together and she had these three home girls that were cute too.

The lyrics in a lot of those songs felt so right. Beyoncé reminded me of older girls in my neighborhood or in school that I wanted to be friends with. She was the cool girl; I wanted to be grown up like her. *Can you pay my bills? Okay, don't worry.* That was badass.

Beyoncé is very aware of the fact that she has different kinds of fans. Even within the Black community she knows that she has Southern fans, she's got fans from up north, from the east coast, the west coast. She knows she's got Caribbean fans. She knows she has gay fans. I can think of times where she has put things in her art for each and every one of those people. For me being of Jamaican descent, hearing her sing "Sister Nancy" at Coachella, I could have cried my whole eyes right out of my face because I was like *What?* I couldn't ask for anything more than that. It's full circle.

I've heard Beyoncé say that when she gets onstage as Sasha Fierce it's almost like she blacks out and she's a totally different person. And she doesn't even remember, half of the time, bits and pieces of the concert because there's just something else that takes over. For me, it's the same when I go onstage to do stand up, although I don't have to remember two hours of choreography and make sure I hit notes and do all of the other things she does fly. But even on some of the darkest days where I'm just feeling like absolute garbage, if you put a microphone in my hand and sit me onstage, I become somebody else. I give myself to my job and to the experience and I allow it to happen. That's Kid Fury.

Beyoncé talks sometimes about being nervous. Even albums and albums into her career she'll be nervous before stepping onstage. You would never think that looking at her; I'm also nervous before every single show. Kid Fury approaches things completely differently than I would. It's really like two different energies—when you're performing versus when you're at the grocery store or at your momma's house. The fact that Beyoncé made a whole album about her alter ego resonates with me.

The things I love and admire the most about Beyoncé are her work ethic and her determination and success in topping herself all the time. I always wonder, what is she going to do next? How is she going to do something bigger than this or better than this or even just as great? And she always does.

Coachella reminded me about one of those aspects that I love about her so much, especially over the past few years, and that is that she has been so blatant and rich in her representation of Blackness. Her Coachella performance was the HBCU experience. She sang the national anthem, she sang "Sister Nancy" like, *I'm going to take it to the Caribbean real quick*. She recognizes not just her Blackness but the importance of being an artist of her stature that is celebrated by people across all racial backgrounds, ethnicities, genders, and sexualities. All those things. People love the art thing, but she recognizes what the narrative is for Black people in this country, especially right now, and she recognizes her power in the platform that she has.

And a lot of artists with platforms—not even as large but just really big ones—are not going to do anything as bold as laying on top of a sinking police car in a music video. Or dressing up like a Black Panther at the Super Bowl. She makes huge statements in her art. It's not always political. Sometimes it's doing a step routine while screaming "suck on my balls" and then twerking. That's plenty Black enough for us. But she's responsible too. She's responsible in the way that she handles her expression and her platform and her art. Nobody walks across the stage like her. Nobody commands a performance like her. Nobody swings their hair around or drops it low like she does. Beyoncé has so many dance numbers. I'm still trying to get the whole Coachella one down. My knees aren't as good as they used to be so I can't get super, super low. But I'm working on it. She has three kids and you would expect by this time she might consider giving up a little bit. That's what you love about her. She will do it pregnant, not pregnant, sick, not sick. She's going to give you a show. Because of that I will always try to keep up with the dances, but I think that "Single Ladies" is the one full routine that I will always know by heart.

The Elevator

---◆---

YLONDA GAULT

Growing up, my beatdown grill intimidated no one. Quite naturally, I mastered the Black girl neck rotation. And in classic "forget-you" fashion, I knew how to flip my wrist with a signifying clap back or two . . . That was all the "fight" I had in me. Yet, everyone knew I was the scrawny lil' brown girl not to be fucked with. My big sister would cut a bitch as sure as she breathed.

I never asked Sissy to defend me. Mama didn't assign her the task. It's just what she did. Fiercely. Girlfriend would *throw down*. Any time. Any place.

From birth, I was a peacemaker. I have a conciliatory disposition that genuinely struggles to comprehend any semblance of aggression. In Mama's words, I "wouldn't say 'shit' if I had a mouth full of it." Sadly, to this day when somebody comes for me, my knee-jerk response is a mix of intellect and empathy—rejoinders, it seems, operate on a two-hour delay. But, my sister? Oh, she ready. Fam burst onto the world with a kind of microprocessing chip that seamlessly converts highly charged emotion into raw combat—with a quickness. No reset. No discourse . . . unless you count her brutal cussing. Once Sissy's earrings come off, run. Because you will lose. Period.

Over the years, she has mellowed. Today, my sister is a grown-ass woman—as am I. And we negotiate life's friction in grown-ass woman fashion. I like to think I've become much better at asserting myself, when necessary. And I don't believe Sissy has greased up to take anybody down in a minute. Still, I know she's got my back. After all this time, there had been little cause for the memories of her Dora Milaje–level protection to surface; they lay quiet and deeply coiled like the tight kinks in my kitchen.

Until . . . The Elevator.

There was a moment—somewhere around the 42-second mark, if you must know—in that oft-played video that sealed the abiding kinship between Beyoncé Knowles-Carter and me. Curious celeb watchers saw many, many things at once: Of course, as Bey later explained, "sometimes shit go down" as it is wont to do "when it's a billion dollars in an elevator." We saw Jay-Z deflecting blow after thunderous blow. And, perhaps, we witnessed the inspiration behind the choreography for their forthcoming "Apesh*t" video. But here is the real deal. That right there was a personal moment for The Queen and me. As she gazed—not just with reverence, but pleasure—at her man's suffering, we were united.

At that 42-second juncture, Bey became real to me. Perfectly so. I no longer saw a cultural icon, a consummately curvy caramel-colored ultimate vision of womanly form. I didn't even see perfectly snatched edges framing poreless skin and 220-gram honey-blond dipped extensions. I honestly believe I saw clear deep to her soul. My heart not only knit into Beyoncé's; I *was* Beyoncé—sorta, kinda, with a short cut, little-ish butt, and B-cup. Like me, she'd clearly been keeping secrets. Hiding behind a sweet-smiled veil of respectability, Bey was as angry and lonely as I. Her marriage was crumbling—as was mine. And only a ride-or-die sister could discern, and in some way attempt to rectify, the years of pain, slights, and outright scorn that had led to its undoing.

Beyoncé is an absurdly talented, international megastar. Physically, she epitomizes our cultural beauty standards, or at least comes about as close as most human specimens can. She is very, very wealthy. She is idolized by millions. And since the late '90s, she has held captive America's celebrity fascination. But life is not that simple.

Because at the end of the after-party, Bey is a Black woman— a Black woman who loves, and is married to, a Black man. And that's a complicated thing. It is a layered and beautiful and rich thing. But it is more than that, because Black love is HARD.

Most assuredly, no billions were at stake in my marriage. More like a paucity of zeros and commas. Still, it was no less unnerving to feel it unravel. It's hard to keep up appearances. But we all do it, especially Black women. We want to be The Good Wife with The Good Husband and The Nice House and

The Cute Kids. We want to look as though we are holding down The Good Job, keeping The Tight Body and rocking The Right 'Do. It's hella work, but we do it with the corners of our mouths turned up—almost reflexively.

Until . . . The Elevator.

Deftly brandishing her copper-colored $1,600 evening bag in a narrow crook of the 35-square-foot cab, Solange Knowles beat Jay-Z like he stole something. Her wiry limbs akimbo, lil' sis smacked, kicked, and scratched Jigga in a fiery display of whoop ass. As stunned as we were by Solange's WWE prowess, none of her moves could compare to the motionless stance of Queen Bey. The careful observer, namely me, took note that Beyoncé lifted nary a meticulously arched eyebrow in her husband's defense. Instead, elegantly turned out in Givenchy couture and a painted-on smile, she stood in tacit support of his flogging. She wanted him to suffer as she had suffered—for years. It was shocking to witness yet, at the same time, eerily familiar.

That day in May 2014, the loop of TMZ's three-minute video footage reverberated through the nation's collective consciousness to startling effect. The Carter-Knowles coupling has been marked by mystery since the two met in or around 1999 . . . or 2000, depending on the celeb rag. Their cloaked marital affairs speak volumes in a maddened celebrity culture so pervasive, the public is updated on intimacies like Gwyneth Paltrow's vagina steams, Gabrielle Union's predilection for booty-licking sex, and everything in between. Even Oprah spills her secrets. Details of the Carter-Knowles coupling, on the other hand, are held down tighter than the al-Qaeda fortress of Tora Bora.

Cultural scholars, pundits, news anchors—even Black Twitter—were nonplussed. The news so transcended tawdry gossip fodder and celebrity clickbait that even esteemed NPR weighed in with deliberate coverage and analysis. "The only thing we *do* know is that we don't know anything at all about what happened," agreed the panelists on Michel Martin's *Tell Me More.*

Yeah . . . nah. I knew. A pop-off like Solange's could mean only one thing. Jay's ass whooping was a long time in the making. Fighters like my sister and Solange, as sudden and savage as their attacks may appear, don't strike without warning. Jay was not being yanked for a single dalliance. I knew the Solange smackdown was cumulative. Just as my sister would have done, Solange had already warned him. On the schoolyard, my sister had a measured but firm way of handling a first or singular offense—circling the miscreant, maybe bumping shoulders. Likely a bit of side-eye at some point . . . a little bit of cussing, soft and slow.

After the first few Beckys, trust me on this, Solange got in bruh-man's face and had words—through clenched teeth and cut-eyed stares—"Look here . . ." She spoke for a good while, making clear his wrongs and the pending consequences. And at some point, as I heard my sister say repeatedly, Solange concluded with words to the effect of: "Mofo, trust and believe! You got one more time to . . ."

Hence . . . The Elevator.

Clearly, past entreaties had failed, leaving Solange no choice. She went HAM. That video had me back on the schoolyard watching my sister bodyslam a pitiless soul on my behalf.

When you have a sis like mine and Bey's, you don't reveal to them each and every slight from a perpetrator. Call it a hunch, sibling intuition—maybe, just mercy. But I know from experience as the pacifist sibling, the sister who loves to brawl will not dole out as many do-overs as I will.

I saw all of the interwebs go *Lemonade* crazy and the world practically bowed at his feet when Jay released a follow-up—admitting his indiscretions on *I Gave You Lemons*. Personally, I didn't need all that "I-Ain't-Sorry, Jealous-or-Crazy," baseball-wielding, yellow-dress-a-flowing hullabaloo. It was entertaining in all its artistry; I'll give you that, but nothing revelatory.

And what I know for sure from her wan smile is that Bey had been saving face for many, many years. Because when you're the "nice" sister, your entire life should be, well . . . nice. And when you are the "peacemaker"—even if only in your own mind—quite naturally you don't want to *disturb* the peace of everyone's perception. That would be messy. It would cause a stir. Be reasonable. If you have a husband who, outwardly, does all the things a husband should do. A husband who looks the part, has a measure of charm, and is not "nearly as bad as a lot of men out there." Just grin and bear it. Things could be a lot worse.

Of course, all of this is pure conjecture on my part. Bey's countenance is what is expected from perfect women. I mean, I *may or may not* be a bit of a pleaser myself. But I do know what it is to do certain things and to not do certain things in a take-one-for-the-team show of support. Somehow, the first time becomes the third and then the seventeenth and then a full-on habit. After all, our brothers have a lot to deal with. Life is easier for us, Black women are taught. We can handle more. Be nice. Smile. Act like it's going well. Figure out how to make him shine. Deny yourself all the pieces of yourself you worked to build. Be pretty. Don't forget nice. And sweet.

Full disclosure: I don't stan for Bey. Never have, really. I'm not sure I even understand or trust the Beyhive. That level of adoration concerns me. Yet, I do *like* and admire Beyoncé . . . a lot. As though it were yesterday, I can remember walking through downtown Brooklyn with "No, No, No" blasting so often it may as well have been my theme song. I heard it from every double-parked jeep on Flatbush Avenue and even in my head when it wasn't playing at all. Way back in the days of Wyclef, Kelly Rowland, LeToya Luckett, and the other booted Child, I remember young Supremes and their stiff press-and-curls. Even before she'd filled out, got a weave, or hired a stylist, Beyoncé took center stage. There was a knowingness behind Beyoncé's eyes that seemed to telescope her superstar status. Solo Bey was not an "if" but a "when." Sounds corny, I know. But it was as though she sensed her destiny.

Until . . . The Elevator.

Seeing her stand witness to her husband's beatdown reminded me of the inner-knowingness that first drew me in. Beyoncé was placed in the elevator, but she was not *in* the elevator; she was someplace else. Only this time her eyes revealed a not-so-promising destiny. There was a sadness and emptiness where there had been hope. The void in her gaze also reminded me that, until that videotaped scuffle, I hadn't been feeling Bey for the past decade or so. We hadn't exactly fallen out. She was more like that good girlfriend you used to hang with but lost track of—haven't seen or heard from in ages.

In hindsight, I never really "got" solo Beyoncé. You know when she went strutting up that alley with the denim booty shorts, red stilettos blowing all of our minds? That was hot, hot, hot! I loved every second of it. And I can't lie, that jam had me twerking in the mirror and "uh-oh-uh-oh-uh-oh-ing" my struggle ass off. As addictive as that breakout single was, I realize now that it was, perhaps, where our relationship became a bit fraught. Damn if it wasn't the most intoxicating tune ever. But I just couldn't help myself; all kinds of confusion was swirling in my head. I wanted to whisper in her ear:

"Why he got *you* looking crazy right now? You're Beyoncé. For real, you *really* hoping he'll page you right now? Save you right now? Why, boo?"

I mean, if Beyoncé is not worthy of a man's full and uncompromised attention, what does that mean for the rest of us? I, for one, wanted to be enough for a man . . . to the point where I didn't need to be out here "looking crazy." I wanted to be enough by my damn self. But I wasn't. And, apparently, neither was the Queen. Funny, she'd somehow led me to believe—or I should say, hope—that I could be like those angels of Charlie's and throw my hands up along with "all the ladies who independent," yet still find true love and support. "Try to control me, boy you get dismissed . . . always fifty-fifty in relationships." Right, B?

Years before she was crazy in love, and later drunk in love, Beyoncé inspired me. As time passed, she entertained me quite nicely with clever dance tracks like "Get Me Bodied" and "Freakum Dress." As a performer, as a pop star, Bey undoubtedly earned her legendary status.

Then, in the time it took to fold her Dereon jeans, she began to change her tune. And by the time she got to "Bow Down," in the early part of 2013, I was outright pissed. I didn't have a problem with a confident Beyoncé proclaiming her eminence . . . all facts. But what was she raging about? And to whom, what coterie of bitches, was Bey's fire directed? The juxtaposition of a rage-fueled tirade against haters with Chimamanda Ngozi Adichie's "We Should All Be Feminists" sampling didn't help matters:

> We teach girls to shrink themselves . . . Otherwise, you would threaten the man . . . marriage can be a source of joy and love and mutual support but why do we teach girls to aspire to marriage and we don't teach boys the same?

Then, to round out the tune, we get more of Beyoncé's aggressive posturing (God damn, God damn!) about waking up like this and how her man made her feel so God damn fine.

I thought it was just me. But it seems Adichie herself had mixed feelings as well, telling a Dutch newspaper that Beyoncé's "type of feminism is not mine." She said of Bey's notion of being a feminist that "it gives quite a lot of space to the necessity of men. I think men are lovely, but I don't think that women should relate everything they do to men: did he hurt me, do I forgive him, did he put a ring on my finger?"

Don't get me wrong. I, too, am a walking contradiction.

And I'm all here for an artist's complexity. I think it is brave of Bey to walk in her creativity. Part of what separates creatives from the rest of the world are the paradoxes that both nurture and torment. We tend to be both smart and naive, a bit cocky but also insecure, equal parts playful and disciplined, at turns extroverted and introverted. Intellectualizing her nuanced persona, though, could not make up for the fact that Bey was beginning to wear on me.

For a stretch of time, I felt as though she was on the verge of overexposure. Remember when she seemed to make as many TV appearances as the NBC peacock? Every. Single. Awards. Show. Let's not forget when she felt a need to bogart the 2015 Grammys, knowing good and well the wildly underrated Ledisi should've had her a Selma "Precious Lord" moment. Funny how Bey, the Oshun goddess, snatched back the Holy Ghost once 25 million viewers were at stake. That was foul. Not unforgivable foul, just odd foul. Like, who *was* she even?

Was the performance an antidote to the spectacle of the previous year's "Drunk in Love"—where she showed her entire ass, on stage simulating sex? Call me what you want. I am not a prude and I am not a hater. But just why was that necessary? Sure, I suppose a middle-of-the-night album drop was genius and all. But I didn't need Beyoncé going on about giving her husband blow jobs. I simply did not need that information. I did not need that visual. And I was also uncomfortable with Jay-Z's "supporting" role in all of it. When he got up on that stage, watching her writhe in front of millions, I nearly lost it. I was screaming, "Dude, get your woman up off the floor; grab her pocketbook; and take y'all asses home!" He didn't hear me though.

He proudly riffed on and on—"If I do say so myself." Then, and here is where it all went completely left: "I'm Ike. Turner turn up/Baby, no, I don't play/ Now, eat the cake Anna Mae/I said, eat the cake, Anna Mae."

So now he's going to liken himself to an abuser? And we're supposed to call that "sexy"? Perhaps you have to be a certain age—okay, old—like me (and Jay) to know about Tina Turner's cake moment. The whole event is explained both in her memoirs and in the movie based on her life, *What's Love Got to Do With It.* Ike Turner, her notoriously abusive manager and husband, gives Tina a verbal lashing in the middle of a restaurant. As their argument escalates, he orders Tina to eat the cake he'd ordered for her. Things turn violent and Ike ends up smashing and smearing the cake all over Tina's face. It's one of those movie scenes that never leaves you.

For the life of me, I couldn't see why the Carters would want to conjure that image . . . like, now we're championing sexual assault? That's how you two get down?

Granted, I can't speak from personal cultural-icon experience. But, to my mind, there has to come a time you no longer have to prove to the world how alluring or provocative you are. We see you, Bey. We been seeing you. So why are you out here doing the most? I was mad.

Until . . . The Elevator.

That 3:32 video loop made sense of everything. What it revealed was a Black woman just as broken, just as strong, just as muddled, just as sure, just as hungry, just as wise, just as lacking, just as complete, just as proud, and just as vulnerable as me.

I love her for that.

The Art of Being Beyoncé

MARIA BRITO

She is crouching, surrounded by poppies, peonies, orchids, and roses in white, pink, burgundy, and yellow. She's staring straight at the camera, not a hint of shyness in her gaze. She is semi-naked, protected by a veil, a belly notably protruding. It's February 1, 2017, and Beyoncé Knowles-Carter has just announced to the world via her own Instagram account that she is pregnant with twins.

The image is highly artistic and enticing; we can't take our eyes off everything that is in it. A few hours later, other photographs from the same series start showing up on her website and then migrate across the internet. We learn that Los Angeles–based, Ethiopian-born artist Awol Erizku has created this portfolio to celebrate and commemorate the announcement. The series is titled "I Have Three Hearts"—inspired by an accompanying poem by Somali-born, London-based Warsan Shire, who also collaborated on the lyrics for *Lemonade*.

The media frenzy is instant, as everyone rushes to deconstruct and decipher every image. For example, the green veil, New York University art historian Dennis Geronimus tells *Harper's Bazaar*, is an homage to Our Lady of Guadalupe, the patroness of the Mexican Catholic Church. Art historian Adrianna Campbell also draws parallels to the work of Mexican artist Frida Kahlo. Frida was a multifaceted woman at the center of her own celebrity and personal hardship, including several miscarriages and a tumultuous marriage to the very high-profile Diego Rivera. It's easy for Beyoncé to feel kinship.

But what's most striking in these images are the references to the Roman goddess of sex, love, and fertility, directly alluding to Sandro Botticelli's fifteenth-century masterpiece "The Birth of Venus." In one of the photographs, Beyoncé is standing naked on a pedestal covered with lush tropical greenery, shielding a breast with one hand, the other holding her belly, while her cascading hair envelopes the side of her body. In another, rendered in black and white, she is sitting on a throne of flowers, her expression more demure, almost virginal. That is, if it weren't for her expanded midriff.

I was about seven months pregnant with my youngest son at the end of 2009. One morning in December I headed for Tracy Anderson's exercise studio in New York City (then in a loft on Hubert Street). I was about to start my daily workout when Beyoncé appeared by my side. More impressively, she saw me. "And how could she not?" my husband said later that day when I told him. Needless to say, I was very noticeable with tight exercise clothes and a gigantic stomach, dancing and contorting in a 90-degree heated room. "B"—also in black leggings and gray tank top, hair up in a ponytail, bare-faced, taller and much more beautiful than in all her pictures and videos—looked at me and my belly with grace, surprise, delight, and a big, warm Southern smile. "Congratulations!" she said, and we bonded, albeit for seconds, over our womanhood. That day it dawned on me that Beyoncé's artistry depends as much on her empathy, her vulnerability, and her humanity as it does on her creativity, all quintessential elements for being a true and lasting artist.

I tell all my clients when I start working with them that contemporary art is always helping us to make sense (or nonsense) of our own selves and our surroundings while keeping the eye, the mind, and the heart engaged: for the viewer there are so many aesthetic elements to enjoy, so many ideas that a piece of art can generate, and so many emotions that can be felt for which words sometimes don't even exist. The art of our times sometimes references the past, sometimes tries to unveil the future, but mostly allows us an opportunity to evaluate the present, and on many occasions, it holds up a mirror where we can see ourselves.

Beyoncé, an art collector herself, told *The New York Times* in a profile about her mother, Tina Lawson, that growing up: "it was important to my mother to surround us with positive, powerful, strong images of African and African American art so that we could reflect and see ourselves in them . . . My mother has always been invested in making women feel beautiful, and her art collection always told the stories of women wanting to do the same." It is not surprising, then, that Beyoncé continues to be inspired by art and make references to it every time she has a meaningful opportunity to do so. Art makes life interesting: music, dance, film, visual arts, and performance share this common denominator. All these art manifestations together or alone enlarge our souls, expand our spirits, give us new perspective. Beyoncé combines them all: in songs, images, concerts, and videos that invite contemplation about the African diaspora, about what it means to be a Black woman in America, or simply what it means to be a woman in today's world.

The ultimate aim of self-expression is an irrepressible need to bridge the gap between one another. The gap that separates us as human beings, that feeling that we all have in our lives at some point or another, that makes us feel misunderstood or alone, can only be closed through our shared universal experiences: those feelings of grief, shame, sexual instinct, joy, sadness, ecstasy, sorrow, fear, euphoria, and love. Artists push innovation and bring new ideas to the forefront by acknowledging the past, sometimes referencing other artists and their artworks, sometimes adding elements like passages from literature, poetry, film, pointing at a sociopolitical movement or highlighting a moment in history. Artists appropriate, transform, reinterpret, reenact, shape-shift, give credit, and pay homage to those who have paved the way before them.

Beyoncé is a master at exactly such quotations. Take, for example, the video of "Mine," released as part of her 2013 eponymous album. Beyoncé moves slowly, the lighting is pure and clean, she wears a heavy veil and a strapless dress that gives the illusion of marble, like the surface of a sculpture. A male model is resting on her lap. It is a direct reference to Michelangelo Buonarroti's "La Pieta," the Carrara marble Renaissance sculpture finished in 1499 and considered one of the greatest works of one of the greatest artists of all time. Later in the video a man and a woman are kissing; their heads are covered with white cloth. They look very much like Belgian surrealist René Magritte's painting "The Lovers." Beyoncé is smoothly mixing Italian Renaissance, surrealism, R&B, and African beats. Talk about modern-day syncretism.

And there's the video of "Hold Up." Every woman who has ever felt mad, betrayed, angry, invalidated, cheated, vengeful, obsessed, or brokenhearted finds catharsis through the visuals and lyrics:

I don't wanna lose my pride, but I'mma fuck me up a bitch

At the crossroads of art, music, fashion, and performance in "Hold Up," Beyoncé draws inspiration from Swiss artist Pipilotti Rist's 1997 double screen "Ever Is Over All," which debuted at that year's Venice Biennale. (Rist has been working in many different mediums since the early 1980s but her impact remains in a niche, as in art collectors, museum-goers, art lovers, and connoisseurs. A Google search of her name will suggest in third place the word "Beyoncé" next to it, because people want to know how contemporary art has influenced Beyoncé, and in the process, they have learned about many artists, Rist being just one of them.) In Rist's work, the artist walks down the street wearing a turquoise dress and red heels while smashing the windows of parked cars with an oversize flower in a gracious and feminine way. In "Hold Up," Beyoncé is wearing a flowing, sexy, organza amber dress and black platforms. With fire on her hips and her characteristic swagger, she swings a baseball bat, shattering car windows, store vitrines, hydrants, and video cameras. For both Rist and Beyoncé it's a paradox: delicate creatures performing aggressive actions while keeping big smiles on their faces.

Afro-Futurism is also part of Beyoncé's favorite visual genre. In the 2016 video for "Sorry," Nigerian artist Laolu Senbanjo painted geometric motifs on the dancers' bodies. He called his paintings the Sacred Art of the Ori, because this practice derives from a spiritual Yoruba ritual. There are clear parallels to the work of Keith Haring and the way he painted on singer Grace Jones's body for her live performance at New York City's Paradise Garage in 1985. Beyoncé's performance at the Grammy Awards in February 2017 right after the announcement of her second pregnancy was also peppered with Afro-Futuristic elements. We see her dressed like a goddess, someone who casts a light into the world as if redeeming the entire Black race. Her dress, created by designer Peter Dundas, was inspired by Gustav Klimt's golden phase, with elaborate Art Deco motifs inspired by Erté. The gilded halo, although Byzantine in its construction and aesthetics, is a nod to Oshun, whose symbolism abounds in Beyoncé's videos and performances. Yellow, gold, and amber are the colors associated with the Yoruba goddess of fecundity, sexuality, beauty, love, luxury, and pleasure, all qualities that she embraces and conspicuously highlights with her fertile body.

Beyoncé and Jay-Z amazed the world when in the summer of 2018 they dropped *Everything Is Love*. The music video for the first promotional track, "Apesh*t," was filmed at the Louvre in Paris. The Carters and their dancers move around the regal galleries of the museum creating contrast and tension between their own bodies as contemporary pop icons and artworks like the Mona Lisa, the Venus de Milo, and the Winged Victory of Samothrace, all identifiable historical treasures that have withstood centuries without losing their appeal. I'm particularly captivated by the scene where Beyoncé is with her troupe of dancers, all women whose body types are very diverse, all Black, and all wearing flesh-toned leotards, leggings, and skimpy tops. They look defiantly straight at the camera under the massive painting by the preeminent French Neoclassical painter Jacques-Louis David, "The Consecration of the Emperor Napoleon I and Coronation of the Empress Josephine in the Cathedral of Notre-Dame de Paris on 2 December 1804," finished by the artist in 1807 after being commissioned directly by Napoleon Bonaparte. The painting depicts the coronation of Napoleon as the emperor of France and of his wife Josephine, in front of Notre Dame's altar and a large group of dignitaries, including Pope Pius VII. What I find amusing, if not subversive, is that Napoleon was described by historians as a misogynist who didn't see women as equal to men and who called them "nothing but machines for producing children." He stripped women of many rights, turning them almost into their husband's property, as written in the pages of his Napoleonic Code. He was an absolutist who censored the press and attempted to control every media that then existed, to turn their words and messages into benevolent propaganda that supported each one of his moves. There is such stark contrast between who Napoleon was and what he represented and the feminist, open-minded, egalitarian, and democratic attitude of Beyoncé, making that scene at the Louvre look and feel like an electric shock to history.

In thinking about her contribution to art and entertainment, to pop culture and to the world at large, I've come to believe that Beyoncé has found a way to give new meaning to the power of the image, intermixing classic with contemporary, western with non-western, the divine with the profane. She has created her own language, dignifying and elevating African Americans, women, and freedom of expression. It is acceptable and even desirable to be sexual, to be curvy, to be a muse of many and a muse to oneself, to love our bodies, to love our husbands, to be devoted mothers, and in Beyoncé's case, to insert herself into the most iconic works of art and to do it tastefully and masterfully in ways that no other performer has ever done. She's a creator whose indelible mark in our culture has earned her a spot in art history.

Grown Women:
A Conversation About
Coming of Age with an Icon

———◆———

MELISSA HARRIS-PERRY AND
MANKAPRR CONTEH

MELISSA HARRIS-PERRY

The coffee mug is a warning. When 5:30 a.m. finds my toes hitting the floor thirty seconds before my heels—like I've slept in stilettos preparing for the slay I will bring to my day—that's when I grab the gold mug with black letters screaming I WOKE UP LIKE THIS. Make way.

When the day refuses to dawn, even well after noon. When my inner Sasha can't find the zip code of fierce—That's when I choose the white mug, with a dishwasher-faded gray message: *I'm suffering a severe case of not being Beyoncé.*

It hasn't always been this way. It is odd that she has become my barometer. I didn't even like Destiny's Child. No shade. But I am twelve years her senior. Little Beyoncé and her friends— "Wait, isn't one her sister?" "Girl, I don't know, turn up that En Vogue!"—just didn't move me.

Then 2003. I was grown. Married. The mother of a brand-new baby girl. Beyoncé was "Crazy in Love." The first time I caught the video I was in the living room. My graduate student was in the kitchen. I screamed out to her, "Dani! Come here. Look at this! Beyoncé got some and it was definitely consensual. And it was definitely good." We watched it again. By the third time we had it memorized. Fifteen years later Dani is no longer my graduate student. She is my faculty colleague. But if the DJ plays "Crazy in Love" we clear the dance floor with a routine perfected through the years.

It is complicated to admit as a feminist scholar, a political scientist, a co-conspirator of queer movements, but it was the sex that drew me. An instant recognition of this girl-to-woman transition. It stirred my embodied memories of the first time sex was wanted and satisfying.

I watched Beyoncé's love madness and grinned like a proud big sister watching her bloom. She was Zora Neale's Janie laying beneath the pear tree as the leaf buds opened. "This singing she heard that had nothing to do with her ears . . . It connected itself with other vaguely felt matters that had struck her outside observation and buried themselves in her flesh."

I was invested in the journey of Beyoncé. She was not me—but rather the niece, the daughter, the student. Younger. Prettier. Far more talented, but connected, so that the youth, beauty, and talent invoke only pride, not competition. First person plural. We. As an aunt, mother, teacher. I read her comfortably—joyously—from this place.

MANKAPRR CONTEH

When *The Writing's on the Wall*, I am five or six. I am definitely not seven. I am in Raleigh, North Carolina, where the sun beams into Auntie Marie and Uncle Sheikh's house like stage lights. My big cousins play music videos. I am proud that I can deduce that "automobills" is a play on words as Black Barbie doll singers prance around a spacey hair salon. Men are in cages. I probably scan the screen, imagining which pop star I can be. I probably want to be Beyoncé. I probably decide to be LeToya.

When Beyoncé is "Dangerously in Love," I am almost a fourth grader.

When she is "Irreplaceable," I am a tortured preteen.

When she is Sasha Fierce I am a sly teen-teen.

When she has "Love on Top," I am a high school senior on the precipice of independence.

Like Morgan Parker's Beyoncés, I am on a desperate quest to be loved—by my teachers, by my parents, by prestigious colleges, by the boys I kiss when their mothers aren't home. I place high stock in being *pretty for a dark-skinned girl*, for I have resolved that I will never be pretty like Beyoncé. I place high stock in being school-smart, because I'll never dance or sing like her. And I'll never be Black like her, either. Our strange three-syllable names come from different worlds. Hers is an homage to her Creole mother's maiden name. Beyoncé belongs to a Black family that has been, at least in part, violently rooted in American soil far longer than the one generation my Sierra Leonean family has spent here at their own will. As a cultural figure, I think Beyoncé belongs to Black girls like her.

I still like the girl, though—I do. In the third or fourth grade, I study the lyrics to "Me, Myself and I" in the shower. In middle school, I audition for the talent show with a tone-deaf rendition of "Say My Name." I buy one short-sleeved black-and-white House of Dereon hoodie littered with fleurs-de-lis. When I get my license, I shake and shimmy and snap my neck to "Countdown" as I whip my dull gold 2001 Toyota Corolla around New Castle County. Still, in my pop culture solar system, Beyoncé is just a star among many, and it's not unusual for me to discount her shine.

"You know, Kelly is really the prettiest."

"Michelle had the best verse on 'Cater 2 U'."

"*B-Day* and *4* are just alright as full albums."

I am more interested in boys and men as performers, and in general. Usher, Kanye, Drake—they are the sun, the moon, the earth. And even with these celebrities at the center of my universe, I have decided I want to be famous for doing something Good, like anchoring news or writing laws or improving Sierra Leone's educational capacity, not twirling around the BET Awards in a silver two-piece.

MELISSA HARRIS-PERRY

What fun to watch her grow!

Look, y'all, did you see it? Baby girl has embraced her feminism. Nah forget that, her FEMINISM. All capital letters, emblazoned lights, fire. With homage to Alice Walker, Beyoncé FEMINISM is to Becky feminism what purple is to lavender.

Look y'all, did you see it? Baby girl brought J-setting to pop music. They think she is just dancing in a black leotard with her girls and have no idea she has run Jackson State Marching Band and queer brothers from the 7th Ward all up into the center of American culture . . . Riiiight!

Look y'all, baby girl is having a baby girl!

Look y'all, baby girl is hanging with POTUS and FLOTUS Obama. And they are the ones star struck.

Look y'all, did you see it? Baby girl just sank a cop car in Katrina floodwaters and went full-on Black Panther at the Super Bowl.

"So what?"

2016. Enter Mankaprr Conteh.

MANKAPRR CONTEH

When Beyoncé stops the world, I am a sophomore at Wake Forest University, working on the being-famous-for-something-Good thing. Too much of the time, I'm thinking about dying. My metallic Corolla has been replaced with a sleek black Honda Civic that I consider careening over an overpass. Beyoncé has the nerve to release an outstanding self-titled hip-pop-n-b visual album on which she *bravely* confesses that being pretty is a problem for her. She is so committed to this confession that she makes "Pretty Hurts" the album's first track and a single. I'm relatively cute and remarkably sad, but the two have little to nothing to do with each other.

My first time listening to *Beyoncé*, I am speeding away from the campus that triggered a dormant and clinical depression, darting north for one month of wintry freedom. This album makes me feel unchained. It wakes my sleepy muscles, my meandering pulse. I am dangerously texting friends about how *good* the music is, and I am giving the driver's seat that work. I am running songs back and singing and shouting and singing and shouting. When I watch the album, I am mesmerized by the detail, the diversity, and the movement of its images. It is the first time I feel like I'm consuming high art in watching music videos. It is the first time I feel like Beyoncé is high art herself.

I think her self-titled album is a musical masterpiece, but see holes in "Bow Down," "***Flawless," and the album as a whole as the feminist manifestos people like Melissa Harris-Perry have declared them. If Beyoncé loves women so much, why is she talking to us so crazy? Who are these bitches she's telling to bow down and what have they done to escape the good graces of Beyoncé's feminism? Does she have to embrace professional competition among women with such disdain for her competitors? Do I not have enough men calling me a bitch? Do I really need one of the most popular entertainers in the world calling me one too?

And am I supposed to feel sexually empowered by a woman with a perfect body, balance, and footwork rolling on a couch in ways I never could? Am I supposed to praise her overt sexuality now that she's waited until she is a wed mother to unleash it?

I have joined a Black sorority, I have been dating a pro-Black nationally ranked debater, and I have begun thinking a lot about womanhood and race—so much so that I ideate and co-organize a forum on "feminism and race in the age of Beyoncé" in the spring. I enlist my Feminist Political Thought professor to interject her expertise as a soror and I ask a classroom of collegiates how they feel about their own feminist sensibilities, about Miley Cyrus's twerking, Olivia Pope's commandeering, Beyoncé's career, and how and why we understand all of them the way we do. We read aloud an open letter to Michelle Obama admonishing her admiration of the pop star. I think the letter is trash. I think Beyoncé is definitely worth talking about, worth admiring, and worth protecting . . . But I also am not ready to emboss my feminist flag with her image.

When we're told to get in "Formation," I am back on campus for a second semester after a one-year hiatus. The year before, it felt like leave or die, so I left. When I return, Melissa Harris-Perry is now a faculty member at Wake Forest.

I am glad I went away to attempt to get my life together the same year she came to campus.

I kind of want to be her.

I am enrolled in her course on the trajectory of Black freedom movements, named for the one of the day: Black Lives Matter.

It is the first class since Beyoncé marched into Levi's Stadium with a Black power militia of dancers gyrating for dear life. It is the first class since Beyoncé's first single and music video in two years was dropped like an anthemic bomb.

Here is Beyoncé rejecting racial ambiguity. To know and love Beyoncé, she insists, is to know and love her man's negro nose, her baby's afro, her Southern roots, her frustration with Black death at the hands of the state.

Dr. Harris-Perry is animated as she details just how incredible, how enlightened, how earthshaking "Formation" is.

I didn't feel the Earth shake, but I feel my voice shake as I go to interrupt her. I think about our class, its name, its content. I say something to the effect of "I just don't think Formation's logic is gonna get us free."

Dr. Harris-Perry had just assigned us *Assata: An Autobiography*. I remember my dad spitting the word "capitalist" out of his mouth like a curse as I grew up. "Damn capitalist country!" he would bark into the ether, perhaps triggered by CNN on the screen, perhaps triggered by a new bill in the mail. Assata Shakur's condemnation of capitalism made my father's bitterness make sense.

But here is Beyoncé, acting like hard work is the key to prosperity, I think and say to Prof. MHP. Here is Beyoncé, encouraging us to ascend to capitalism's nearly impossible heights rather than break down its oppressive walls. Here is Beyoncé, immediately selling "Formation" memorabilia that is likely pricey for the communities the video showcases and likely produced by poor people across the globe, as I imagine her Ivy Park line is. The best revenge against white supremacy is not, and will never be, succeeding at the capitalist game. Because capitalism, in which players seek the highest profit at the lowest cost to them, will always exploit people and resources.

And while I sincerely believe Beyoncé cares about state violence against Black people, that she does want the police to stop killing us, I cannot shake the feeling that she waited to say so until it was popular—until it was safe for her image and pockets. I find "Formation" to take a rather center-left position while its performer has the social and material capital to go further.

MELISSA HARRIS-PERRY

In 2003 I called my beloved student to witness Beyoncé's transformation. Dani and I have been dancing ever since. For more than a decade I called readers and viewers to witness, analyze, applaud, and appreciate the mastery of King Beyoncé. All came. Joined the potluck. Brought dishes to the table. Feasted on her magnificence.

All these years later I'd once again called my students to the table, but one would not join. Mankaprr pushed back, looking a bit disgusted but mostly disinterested. A lifetime vegan offered steak and potatoes. "I suppose I see why other people might find it nourishing, but it does nothing for me."

Mankaprr is sitting in front of me. All hair. And skin. And

legs. And genius. And pulsating courageous soul. Sitting at my table but rejecting my meal.

I'm irritated. And fascinated. I ask her to write.

She never stops.

MANKAPRR CONTEH

Right before we first taste *Lemonade*, I am happy. I am full of purpose and hope and excitement and light. I am working as a communications intern for Dr. Harris-Perry's Anna Julia Cooper Center for intersectional scholarship. I have been whisked away to Debra Lee's house for the BET Honors. I have sparred with Arsenio Hall and taken selfies with Eric Holder and chatted up a reporter for the *Washington Post*. I am glad I've kept my Honda Civic on the road.

I am in a Virginia Beach hotel room with a younger soror, avoiding our organization's regional conference activities, the night the HBO special premieres. The world is abuzz with anticipation. I catch the end of it, more out of curiosity than excitement. I am impressed, but isn't Beyoncé always impressive?

After it goes off the air, my best girlfriend Camry tells me that Beyoncé's film made her cry. I am intrigued, because in our four years of friendship, I had never seen her shed a tear.

Then, the next day, Dr. Harris-Perry asks us to write. She is compiling a roundtable on *Lemonade* for ELLE.com and wants Camry and me to contribute to it. It is my first opportunity to be published in a national outlet—in any outlet outside of my school newspaper. We stay up all night in the basement of Wake Forest's lofty business school, rigging up our laptop to a projector, playing *Lemonade* through Prof. MHP's husband's Tidal account.

And I finally see my world, my goals, and myself in Beyoncé's art.

MELISSA HARRIS-PERRY

2016 was the hardest of my adult life. The bitterness of what was taken sat in my mouth like the sour metal of an enslaving bit. So much to say. I am screaming. But no one can hear me anymore. People greet me as though I am a ghost at my own funeral. "We miss you." But I am here! "So sorry you are gone." I am standing right here! No one noticed. Pretty girl meet invisibility. Smart girl meet deaf ears.

I inched toward the edge. Unwilling to choose the faded mug every day. Then Beyoncé and Mankaprr began co-creating.

Bey made *Lemonade* and folded time. Sat me in the student's seat and chose the role of teacher. Bey and I stood together on the ledge. How had she known that in my darkness I daily wondered what it would feel like to jump? How long would it take to fall? Would it hurt when I came to the ground? Beyoncé took my hand. Showed me. First person plural. We jumped. We fell into the waters instead.

Beyoncé flipped the classroom. Took Socratic authorship. Forced the questions. What would happen if we took the hopes, dreams, pain, joy, loss, bodies, voices, stories, expressions, styles, families, histories, futures of Black girls and women and put them in the center and started from there?

Made me whisper in response—*Lemonade* happens.

But I was off balance. The sour in my mouth so strong I wanted to add too much sugar, I no longer knew what *Lemonade* should taste like. I called the squad. The *Lemonade* roundtable. Mankaprr writes. I am reading Mankaprr. Learning. I think I am beginning to understand, but I am still missing it.

MANKAPRR CONTEH

I see that Beyoncé's pain may not look like mine, like self-loathing, like guilt, like paralyzing anxiety. It looks like heart-break, resentment, and like the sturdy ground of Christian monogamy being pulled from beneath her, as Professor Blair L. M. Kelley points out. Pain she let us all see.

Then, Beyoncé portrayed all kinds of pain, pain that was not her own.

"When a little dark-skinned girl looks at Beyoncé longingly in 'Accountability' under a voice-over of Bey reciting the line 'You look nothing like your mother,' she acknowledges the colorism that haunts us," I write for Prof. MHP, for ELLE.com.

In that moment in *Lemonade*, it feels like Beyoncé wants me to know she understands my subconscious resentment, that it makes sense, that it is valid, that pretty may hurt her, but it helps her so much too.

"In jumping to her death, she confronts the reality of suicide among us," I go on to say.

Us, yes, but me. Me. To see Beyoncé act out my dark fantasy in *Lemonade*, to think it is a dull daydream she may have had herself, to watch Beyoncé slip on that stigma like a negligee is overwhelming. Is freeing.

"Over and over again, *Lemonade* reminded us of the intertwined, continuous, diasporic suffering of Black folk. When I saw a woman in a southern-gothic dress made of West African Ankara fabric overlooking the newly renovated Superdome, my heart dropped. 'The past and the future merge,' Queen Bey had foreshadowed earlier. No one image better captured the heartbreaking truth of that line. The violence of colonialism in Africa, of the enslavement of West Africans, of the dehumanization of their ancestors in Katrina, and of our continued erasure through capitalism and gentrification—all depicted in mere seconds," I add to the roundtable.

To think Beyoncé did all this in an album perhaps motivated by her husband's transgressions; to think that she expanded her sorrow to generations of strife, and to think she lent her power to all of us, to women across shade and class and Blackness, is to think things I never thought I would think about Beyoncé.

MELISSA HARRIS-PERRY

I have made this mistake before. I have thought the divide was generational. Or regional. Or socioeconomic. When all along I was blinded by my own high yellow privilege. Let me tell you how many times my BFF has gotten me into "Formation" about this particular redbone madness. I kept missing the brown girl pain of genius Mankaprr. I miss it and I see it. I know Mankaprr wants to jump too.

I pray the prayers you are not allowed to pray. I make deals. I wish for all the sour. Leave her the sweet. But I am like Bey. Lemon yellow. Stinging when we mean to soothe. I keep missing it. Even as Beyoncé kept inching closer to getting it right.

And so it happened—that when the pomping and circum-stancing, Divine 9 repping, Drum Major high stepping, and Lifting Every Voice to Sing burst forth through Beychella it was Mankaprr, not me, who sent the invitation to the table. A message in the middle of the night. "MHP, tell me you are watching this."

"When Everything Is Love."

MANKAPRR CONTEH

I watch Beychella in the wee hours of the morning with the energy of the late afternoon. I rejoice and hug my girlfriend Neicy as Bey turns the main stage of the country's most no-torious music festival into an HBCU homecoming. I am so entertained and so moved that *I* cry. I join the ranks of people across gender that know she has just done something defini-tively important.

"Look at what happened when this Black woman had nearly a year to play with thought, to dance with fantasy, to world-build," I write for ELLE.com, for MHP once again. "Maybe, as Beyoncé dreamt of what she wanted to create for this society, she dreamt of what she wanted this society to give her babies: knowledge, pride in identity, deep joy, and freedom, freedom. Perhaps, less abstractly, she simply dreamt of her babies having the sorts of experiences she never had—here, Black collegiate experiences—as parents are wont to do. Regardless, Beyoncé's dreams led her to navigate the institutions Black people have built in pursuit of knowledge, joy, and freedom. As I reflect on how I swayed and twerked and whined and cried to her performance, as I think about what it felt like to revel in untethered bliss, I can't help but think what I felt, in that moment, was liberation. And I can't help but think Beyoncé wants Black people to know liberation is in our reach if we continue to dream of it."

MELISSA HARRIS-PERRY

Beyoncé has won Mankaprr. She has won her with brown girl dreams that show love to her people, remember her past, point toward her future, dance with her sister, and sing with her man. Bey has won Mankaprr, only child of African immigrant parents, by dreaming a brown girl college dream for her new babies. Then following it up with a scholarship fund. Of course.

I read the text. Call the *Lemonade* roundtable. Invite them all to write. But in truth it is not me who has called it. This time, it is Mankaprr. I just got the byline.

And that is when I realize my loyalty shifted. I am still Beyhive. Platinum lifetime member. Forever. But fifteen years after she won me with "Crazy in Love," I watched "Apesh*t" with a certain detachment. Smiled, but wasn't moved. No need to write. If there are words to be written they will come from Mankaprr.

MANKAPRR CONTEH

I still watch "Apesh*t" and wonder what it could have meant and done for Black culture if Beyoncé had shot it at a Black museum rather than the Louvre, but I get why she did it. I get that she wanted to say that we are more beautiful, more valuable, than anything in there.

I wonder what it would have meant for Beyoncé to make protest music after the killings of Amadou Diallo or Sean Bell or Oscar Grant or Aiyana Stanley-Jones; but I get that perhaps, she, like many of us—like me—did not become truly outraged until George Zimmerman was not found guilty of the murder of Trayvon Martin. I think about the over $1.5 million she and Jay-Z have funneled into the Black Lives Matter movement. I think about the way she included Sybrina Fulton, Lezley McSpadden, and Gwen Carr in *Lemonade*, in all their regality and suffering.

I wonder what it would have meant if Beyoncé had given each of the Formation and Homecoming Scholars full rides at their universities as opposed to $25,000 each; I wonder if she could have given more than twelve awards.

But, I get it.

And that's where I am with Beyoncé. I finally get it. I get that she operates within the confines of capitalism; I get that she didn't sign up for destroying them. I get that she wants her children's children's children's children to be incredibly well off; I get that she likely wants that as much as she wants freedom for all of us. I get what she means to lots of Black women, to women I care for deeply. I get what she means to lots of Black people. I get what she means to me. I still don't want to be a pop star, but I get that Beyoncé is, in fact, famous for something Good.

MELISSA HARRIS-PERRY

Beyoncé's gift is greater even than I imagined. She tied me not to herself—but to the journey. Invested me in the talent. The dance. The creation of the world. Bey makes the world. I loved it. Mankaprr unmade it and remade it.

This is the substance of brown girls dreaming: Jacqueline Woodson recounts it in her 2014 memoir *Brown Girl Dreaming*:

> *I cannot write a word yet but at three*
> *I now know the letter J*
> *love the way it curves into a hook*
> *that I carefully top with a straight hat*
> *the way my sister has taught me to do. Love*
> *the sound of the letter and the promise*

that one day this will be connected to a full name,
My own
That I will be able to write
by myself
Without my sister's hand over mine.

What Beyoncé

Means to Everyone

————•————

MEREDITH BROUSSARD
WITH VISUALIZATIONS BY ANDREW
HARVARD AND JUAN CARLOS MORA

The Definitive Beyoncé Biography
ACCORDING TO WIKIPEDIA

Most of my personal milestones have a Beyoncé song as the soundtrack in my memories. I listened to "Crazy in Love" non-stop as I planned my wedding. When I became a mom, "Single Ladies (Put a Ring on It)" was a monster hit among the toddler set, my son included. He and I watched instructional videos of how to do Beyoncé's moves in the video, collapsing

in laughter as we tried and failed to dance like her. That moment was one of the very first times that he and I discovered a shared interest.

As I thought about how Beyoncé has been a constant presence in my own life, I wondered what data analysis could reveal about what she means to other people. (I'm a data journalist; I always wonder how to quantify things.)

First, I turned to Wikipedia. The Wikipedia history of Beyoncé's life is like a peek into the collective unconscious of how other people think about Beyoncé. Wikipedians divide Bey's life into eras based on her albums. Reading about her milestones, it's clear that every stage of her career has brought her exponentially greater success—and that she has been in charge every step of the way. How she has managed her career is an inspiration as I think about what I want my own life to be in the future.

1981: BIRTH OF A QUEEN

SEPT 1981

Beyoncé Giselle Knowles was born on September 4 in Houston, Texas, to parents Tina and Mathew Knowles.

1997–2001: *DESTINY'S CHILD*

FEB 1998

Destiny's Child released its self-titled debut album.

JUL 1999

Destiny's Child released its second studio album, *The Writing's on the Wall*, which Billboard has ranked #39 in its Top 200 Albums of the Decade.

FEB 2001

Beyoncé won her first Grammy with Destiny's Child for "Say My Name" at the 43rd Annual Grammy Awards.

MAY 2001

Destiny's Child released *Survivor*, which debuted at #1 on the U.S. Billboard 200.

OCT 2001

Destiny's Child went on hiatus.

2002–2005: *DANGEROUSLY IN LOVE*

JUL 2002

Beyoncé starred as Foxxy Cleopatra alongside Mike Myers in the hit movie *Austin Powers in Goldmember*, showing the world that she can act as well as sing and dance like a dream.

JUN 2003

Dangerously in Love, Beyoncé's first solo album, launched. The album's lead single, "Crazy in Love," featuring Jay-Z, became Beyoncé's first #1 single as a solo artist in the United States.

FEB 2004

On February 1, Beyoncé performed the American national anthem at Super Bowl XXXVIII in her hometown of Houston, Texas. A week later, she earned five awards at the 46th Annual Grammy Awards, putting her well on her way to becoming one of the most-decorated recording artists of all time.

NOV 2004

Destiny's Child fulfilled its destiny by releasing its final studio album, *Destiny Fulfilled*.

DEC 2005

Beyoncé was nominated for a Golden Globe award for her role in *Dreamgirls* alongside Jennifer Hudson, Jamie Foxx, and Eddie Murphy.

2006–2007: *B'DAY*

SEPT 2006

Beyoncé released her second solo album, *B'Day*, on her twenty-fifth birthday.

2008–2010: *I AM . . . SASHA FIERCE*

APR 2008

On 4/4, Beyoncé married Jay-Z.

OCT 2008

I Am . . . Sasha Fierce dropped on November 18, with the listening party on October 22. Beyoncé shot the video for its monster hit song "Single Ladies (Put a Ring on It)" on what was a scorching hot day in New York City, in a studio without air-conditioning. #hot

JAN 2009

Beyoncé performed at President Barack Obama's first inaugural ball.

MAR 2010

Beyoncé and her mother, Tina Knowles, opened The Beyoncé Cosmetology Center at Phoenix House Career Academy in Brooklyn, a training center for women and men in treatment for drug addiction. Beyoncé also took a nine-month break from performing, her longest hiatus ever.

2011–2012: *4*

JUN 2011

Beyoncé released her fourth studio album, *4*.

JUL 2011

Beyoncé wrote an essay, "Eat, Play, Love," for *Essence* about her 2010 career break. The piece won a writing award from the New York Association of Black Journalists.

JAN 2012

Beyoncé gave birth to her first child, Blue Ivy Carter.

2013–2014: *BEYONCÉ*

JAN 2013

Beyoncé performed at President Obama's second inauguration in Washington, D.C.

FEB 2013

Beyoncé performed at the Super Bowl XLVII halftime show, held at the Mercedes-Benz Superdome in New Orleans.

Life Is But a Dream, a feature-length documentary film about and co-directed by Beyoncé, aired on HBO.

APR 2013

The Mrs. Carter Show World Tour began on April 15. The 132-date tour began in Serbia.

DEC 2013

Beyoncé released her fifth album without warning, and straight to iTunes, much to the surprise of her fans.

APR 2014

Beyoncé and husband, Jay-Z, announced their On the Run Tour, the first time they headlined a stadium tour together.

2016–2017: *LEMONADE*

FEB 2016

The release of "Formation" was another surprise for fans: Beyoncé made it available exclusively on her music streaming platform, Tidal. The first live performance of "Formation" was at the halftime show at that year's Super Bowl L.

APR 2016

Beyoncé released *Lemonade*, an album and a one-hour HBO film. It broke a new record: the most-streamed album in one week by a female artist, due to fans streaming the album on Tidal 115 million times. It sold 1.554 million copies in the United States and became the best-selling album of the year worldwide with global sales of 2.5 million.

JUN 2017

Beyoncé gave birth to twins Rumi and Sir Carter.

SEPT 2017

Beyoncé collaborated with J. Balvin and Willy William to release a remix of the song "Mi Gente," with proceeds from the song donated to those affected by Hurricane Harvey and Hurricane Irma in Texas, Mexico, Puerto Rico, and other Caribbean islands.

2018: *EVERYTHING IS LOVE*

APR 2018

Beyoncé headlined the Coachella Music Festival. The video of her performance on YouTube became the most-watched live performance on that website of all time.

JUN 2018

Beyoncé and Jay-Z released their first joint studio album, *Everything Is Love*, at the start of their On the Run II tour. The album was a surprise drop, released on Tidal and announced with a message "Album out now" onscreen as they ended a London performance. The first video, for the single "Apesh*t," was shot at the Louvre and features the couple standing alone with the world's most famous painting, the Mona Lisa. The symbolism is clear: Beyoncé is as much a part of our collective cultural consciousness as da Vinci.

Searching for Beyoncé

Google collects everything that people type into the Google Search box, and the Google Trends tool shows what people are searching for.* Often, they are looking for Queen Bey. These two charts show Google Trends data on where and when the world becomes a Beyhive.

---

* Google Trends changed its geographical assignment method after January 2011 and changed its data collection method after August 2017. Values of 100 in the chart on the left indicate peak popularity in search interest relative to the highest point on the chart for the given region and time.

The chart on the left shows U.S. states ordered by their interest in searching for the term "Beyoncé." The chart on the right shows when searches for Beyoncé peaked. Generally, these peaks correspond to newsworthy events in Bey's life—the same events that Wikipedians chronicle. It's as if the big moments in Beyoncé's life are shared by millions of people.

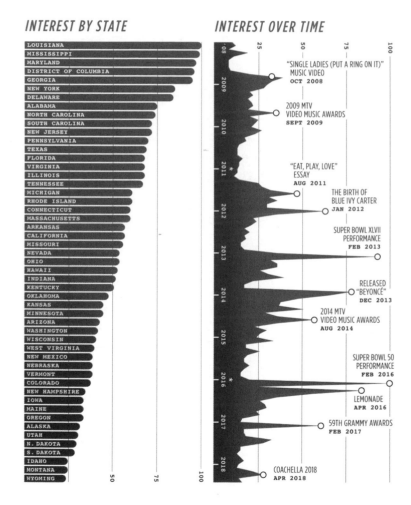

INTEREST BY STATE

LOUISIANA
MISSISSIPPI
MARYLAND
DISTRICT OF COLUMBIA
GEORGIA
NEW YORK
DELAWARE
ALABAMA
NORTH CAROLINA
SOUTH CAROLINA
NEW JERSEY
PENNSYLVANIA
TEXAS
FLORIDA
VIRGINIA
ILLINOIS
TENNESSEE
MICHIGAN
RHODE ISLAND
CONNECTICUT
MASSACHUSETTS
ARKANSAS
CALIFORNIA
MISSOURI
NEVADA
OHIO
HAWAII
INDIANA
KENTUCKY
OKLAHOMA
KANSAS
MINNESOTA
ARIZONA
WASHINGTON
WISCONSIN
WEST VIRGINIA
NEW MEXICO
NEBRASKA
VERMONT
COLORADO
NEW HAMPSHIRE
IOWA
MAINE
OREGON
ALASKA
UTAH
N. DAKOTA
S. DAKOTA
IDAHO
MONTANA
WYOMING

INTEREST OVER TIME

"SINGLE LADIES (PUT A RING ON IT)"
MUSIC VIDEO
OCT 2008

2009 MTV
VIDEO MUSIC AWARDS
SEPT 2009

"EAT, PLAY, LOVE"
ESSAY
AUG 2011

THE BIRTH OF
BLUE IVY CARTER
JAN 2012

SUPER BOWL XLVII
PERFORMANCE
FEB 2013

RELEASED
"BEYONCÉ"
DEC 2013

2014 MTV
VIDEO MUSIC AWARDS
AUG 2014

SUPER BOWL 50
PERFORMANCE
FEB 2016

LEMONADE
APR 2016

59TH GRAMMY AWARDS
FEB 2017

COACHELLA 2018
APR 2018

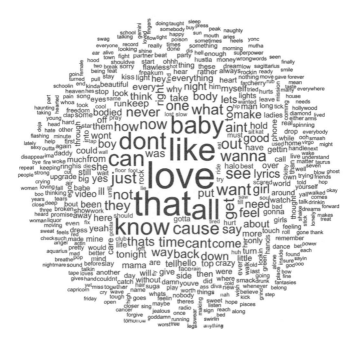

Which Words Appear Most Often in Beyoncé's Songs?

Bey's distinctive, velvety voice is recognizable in an instant; there's no other singer like her. But what about the words in her songs? Is there something that makes them distinctive?

I analyzed all of the lyrics of her songs to find the 500 words that show up most frequently. The word Beyoncé sings most often is "love," which appears 460 times in her songs. The title of her joint album with Jay-Z, *Everything Is Love*, is no accident. Perhaps this is the key to understanding what Beyoncé means to all of us. We listen to Beyoncé because she helps us understand love, and love is what gives life meaning.

Beyonce introduces Blue Ivy to the world in this picture released on Tumblr in 2012

Beyoncé, Influencer

ELODIE MAILLIET STORM[*]

It had been a month since Beyoncé gave birth to Blue Ivy in January 2012. There were no pictures yet, just the baby's first cries recorded on Jay-Z's latest track. What would the fruit of the good girl gone badass musical queen and of the bad boy turned music mogul look like? Whom would she take after? What would she, heiress to fashion royalty, be wearing in her first pictures?

The baby celebrity pictures market had been heating up after Angelina Jolie and Brad Pitt had auctioned off the first images of their baby Shiloh. The transaction reached a reported $4 million, to *People* magazine, in 2005. The first images of their twins, Vivienne and Knox, topped it in 2008, with a reported $14 million, all given to charities.

---

[*] Except as noted, all photos from Beyoncé Knowles / Instagram

Would Blue Ivy command a higher fee?

Who would get the exclusive? *People*? *Vanity Fair*? *Vogue* maybe?

None of the above.

This time there would be no expensive shoot involving baby props, intensive styling, multiple setups, or Annie Leibovitz. There would be no multimillion-dollar advances given to charities.

There it was. A simple hospital picture released for free, using Tumblr, a rising platform at the time.

The picture was sweet and unusually mundane. The quality of the composition was questionable yet endearing. Beyoncé looked radiant and happy but her face was out of focus. Blue Ivy was awake, most likely wiggling. She was suspended in an awkward pose with one arm raised. The background was busy with chairs and a binky. It was like a typical family snapshot—except mom was having a really good hair day, appeared well rested, and had time to apply makeup.

Pedestrian as it might appear, this very personal image marked a profound shift in the overall media ecosystem. Suddenly, celebrities did not need *People* or *Access Hollywood* to promote themselves. They reached their audiences directly through social media, where they shared the most intimate details of their lives. In doing so, they helped accelerate the disintermediation of the press in favor of platforms.

This change also affected the aesthetics of celebrity imagery. It started moving away from the highly stylized, carefully composed, and at times too heavily retouched portraits we had seen gracing the cover of magazines so uniformly for the last two decades.

This does not mean that Instagram and Facebook have liberated Hollywood from tight image control. In some ways, they have had the opposite effect: establishing self-censorship as the norm. Any real friend will ask for your green light before posting a picture of you.

At the time of writing this essay, Beyoncé has 118 million followers on Instagram, which appears to be her platform of choice, most likely because of its highly visual nature. Beyoncé's direct audience engagement has been a key factor in the success of her last three album releases, where surprise and coordination were important tactics.

According to D'Marie Analytics, Beyoncé was the most influential social media celebrity in 2017 and her Instagram posts are worth over $1,000,000 each in advertising value. With 1,637 posts so far on Instagram, even if she charged endorsement fees for only a tenth of them, that would equate to $100 million in advertising value. The following 2013 Warhol-inspired Instagram Pepsi post, which appeared on her feed a year after she released Blue Ivy's image on Tumblr, was part of a $50 million advertising deal Beyoncé struck with Pepsi in 2012. The value is grounded in her brand and image but also most certainly in her direct reach to a wide and very engaged audience.

On her side, Beyoncé put creative control at the center of the reason for the Pepsi partnership. "As a businesswoman, this allows me to work with a lifestyle brand with no compromise and without sacrificing my creativity." The multiyear $50 million commitment was meant to fund the singer's chosen creative projects such as events, photo shoots, or almost anything else, according to the *New York Times*.

She's not just the model, she's become the medium itself.

Interestingly, outside of this very obvious Pepsi post, almost none of Beyoncé's Instagram images are captioned, leaving the commercial intent as a hint. In the next image, the bags are fairly recognizable as Gucci, but the brand is not stated anywhere.

It is not known who photographs Beyoncé on a daily basis, but it is pretty clear that every aspect of her life is documented. In one image, Jay-Z is seen photographing her, and he might be at the origin of a few of those posts. Refinery29 has noted:

When Jay Z isn't moonlighting as a rapper, he has a permanent residency as the world's most sought-after Instagram Husband. Shawn Carter has been dropping hints about his side hustle for years. "When I was talking Instagram / Last thing you wanted was your picture snapped," he explained in *Magna Carta Holy Grail*'s "Somewhere in America."

A *GQ* article noted that Beyoncé has an archive in her office space of every image ever taken of her. As the writer noted, "There, across from the narrow conference room in which you are interviewing her, is another long, narrow room that contains the official Beyoncé archive, a temperature-controlled digital-storage facility that contains virtually every existing photograph of her, starting with the very first frames taken of Destiny's Child, the '90s girl group she once fronted; every interview she's ever done; every video of every show she's ever performed; every diary entry she's ever recorded while looking into the unblinking eye of her laptop."

Whoever the photographer(s), one thing is clear: there is a world between Beyoncé's first image posted on Tumblr, a family snapshot, and her last birth announcement of the twins.

In the first image, she was letting the audience peek into a private moment, using intimacy to get her audience closer, building a relationship. A picture of fragile happiness.

The second birth announcement is the projection of an icon. Much more of a "look at me" moment, carefully thought out, staged, a dialogue with the art world. This is how she decides to project the vision of herself as a mother: an artist with full creative power. A Virgin Mary and Madonna all at once.

It's significant that Beyoncé's first Instagram post was on November 6, 2012, the day that Barack Obama won his second term as POTUS. Her very first post (under the name "Baddie Bey") was of her in a T-shirt that said, "Texans for Obama." *New York Magazine*'s The Cut noted: "After Obama's win was announced, she posted a second photo of a handwritten note that read 'Take that, Mitches,' in reference to the Republican candidate, Mitt Romney, but she quickly deleted it. Five years later, it's the only public social media slipup she's ever made— if you can even call it that." The magazine declared that "Beyoncé Is the Leonardo da Vinci of Instagram."

In the early days, Beyoncé showed herself as a student of the arts. We frequently saw images of her at galleries or museums. Works of art often appeared in her feed. There she was at the Louvre in October 2014 looking at *La Joconde*, years before her latest Louvre music video.

She then proceeded to become the work of art itself. She showed a great affinity for Warhol on multiple occasions, including her posting of playful multiple/mirror images of herself in her feed. As Mashable noted in 2017, "Imagine the power of 16 Beyoncés. Just picture it. You could supply strong, probably renewable energy to a continent with that kind of power. And now we've got a visual."

With the demise of fashion magazines, she shows a path forward for fashion photography in that medium, in her own channels, and in the form of highly creative videos. They are like mini music videos but focusing on Bey's style.

In 2018, she shot the video for "Apesh*t" in the Louvre, and her wardrobe was a literal representation of iconic pieces in the museum. Art historian Theodore Barrow has noted about the similarity of Beyoncé to Marie-Guillemine Benoist's 1800 painting *Portrait of a Black Woman (La Negresse)*: "It is, in fact, a pretty rare depiction of a beautiful black woman in a mode that is closely tied to not only the depiction of the seated virgin Mary but also to mythological goddesses."

Later in 2018, Bey's September 2018 cover of *Vogue* bore resemblance to Jacques-Louis David's 1783 *A Vestal Virgin Crowned with Flowers.*

Tyler Mitchell / Vogue

Beyoncé's carefully constructed image acknowledged both the ways that her fans view her as being a goddess and the ways in which she encouraged her female fans to embrace their divine feminine.

We can see in her use of social media the coming of age of an icon, one who remembers a youth without Twitter or Snapchat or Insta, but who is old enough and savvy enough to master and rework the platforms.

What we lose in the evolution of Beyoncé's Instagram is the original intimacy of the relationship—we loved pulling the curtain back a little bit. But even though we don't feel as close, we gain in the rich insights of her visual construct. As

Jenna Wortham wrote in the *New York Times Magazine*: "Social media has, in its own way, provided us a means of generating other selves. We just haven't yet learned to set them free. Beyoncé has, in her own way. The Beyoncé we follow seems to live and breathe, and provokes a real emotional reaction. It's an illusion that feels intimate and real, a hologram self for us to interact with that, in theory, provides the actual Beyoncé space to exist away from our prying eyes."

The supreme sense of control Beyoncé has taken with her visuals is an interesting counterpoint to the #metoo movement. One can only imagine that as a very young artist, Beyoncé observed the pitfalls that a woman artist might fall into when the men in her professional life controlled the image. Whether she is mirroring a favorite painting, posing with her family, or flashing a fashion-forward look, there is never a sense that Beyoncé is ever doing or showing something she doesn't want to do. It's worth noting that Instagram, as a platform, is only seven years old. Tumblr, Beyoncé's platform of choice before Insta, is only 11 years old. But Beyoncé herself has been in the public eye for more than two decades. In *Freedom*, her duet with Kendrick Lamar, she sings: "I break chains all by myself . . . I'ma keep running 'cause a winner don't quit on themselves." In a very short time, she has broken the media chains that kept an artist from interacting with their fans directly. As she told *Elle* magazine in 2016, "To me, power is making things happen without asking for permission. It's affecting the way people perceive themselves and the world around them." It is, astonishingly, still a rare thing to watch a woman and an artist move through the world with as much power— and the lack of wanting or needing permission—as Beyoncé.

The King of Pop and the
Queen of Everything

———◆———

MICHAEL ERIC DYSON

Beyoncé symbolically snatched from Michael Jackson the crown of best entertainer on the globe, ever, when, ironically enough, the curls atop her glorious crown got snatched into the blades of an electric fan. While that event had hardly anything to do with her ascent, it certainly had a lot to do with the performance of a Black and female identity that could meet any challenge on any stage at any time as she maintained her dignity and cool.

Sure, a fateful elevator would descend in her future, in which she proved the same point, but that was a different stage with very different stakes. And yes, she had stumbled and fallen down a set of stairs six years before her hair got entangled in the fan, but that was long before she became a global icon who would revolutionize the music industry with the release of two monumental visual albums, *Beyoncé* and *Lemonade*, without so much as a peep that they were on the way.

There, in Montreal, Canada, on July 22, 2013, at the Bell Centre, on the North American leg of her Mrs. Carter world tour, in the same year she released *Beyoncé*, Beyoncé's golden locks got caught in a circular high-powered fan as she descended stairs during an encore performance to get closer to her adoring audience. As she continued belting the tune "Halo," Beyoncé's bodyguard, Julius de Boer, tugged at the tufts of hair lodged in the screen of the fan, attempting to dislodge his most famous client's tresses at the very moment she mouthed the lyrics that gravity "can't forget / To pull me back to the ground again." De Boer was joined by a man and a woman from a security detail; the man handed de Boer a sharp implement and he was able, finally, to free Beyoncé from the fan's remorseless suction. Beyoncé didn't miss a note and kept singing throughout, and once free, received a hearty applause from her fans. She even parodied her predicament when she posted on her Instagram account rewritten lyrics to the song, changing them from "It's like I've been awakened / Every rule I've had you breakin'" to "I felt my hair was yankin' / From the fan that's always hatin'."

In case it's not clear, my saying that she got caught in a fan while showing love for the fans who adore her is not simply a clever literary homage to homonyms and puns. And it's more than the truism that her hair symbolizes her crown; it's that her mane is a metaphor, maybe even a metonym, for how often women, doing encores, which means working overtime, are sliced by patriarchy and sexism as they do twice the work of men and get only half the credit. It's not even that Beyoncé and Michael Jackson are an update of the gender inequality spotlighted in a 1982 *Frank and Ernest* cartoon, which was memorably paraphrased by the late maverick treasurer, and then governor of Texas, Ann Richards, when she said to the 1988 Democratic National Convention, "Ginger Rogers did everything that Fred Astaire did. She just did it backwards and in high heels." Beyoncé is not simply doing at a higher level what Michael Jackson so brilliantly did. She's doing what no one before her has done. She is a cunning master who leaves others in her trail, whether she is singing, dancing, or performing. Michael's musical body of work is unrivaled, but Beyoncé's work of her musical body on stage and in videos as a singer-dancer-performer is unsurpassed.

Beyoncé and Michael seemed to share a kinetic performance gene passed on to them by brilliant Black bodies in motion, from Bill "Bojangles" Robinson to Josephine Baker, from Sammy Davis, Jr., to Katherine Dunham. Beyoncé saw her first concert in April 1988 at the age of six when she witnessed Michael Jackson perform at the Summit in Houston, Texas. As a budding artist, Beyoncé spent countless hours absorbing Michael Jackson videos, gleaning dance moves and ideas and a grammar of elastic and electrifying entertainment. Michael Jackson's magnetic performances featured a lean frame that articulated a fluid esthetic of clean lines and mathematically precise gestures that Beyoncé embraced in her own repertoire. But she upped the ante. As she matured, Beyoncé expanded the vocabulary of motion with a voluptuous frame that accentuates a combustible physical expressiveness and a more intense poetry of flexibility.

Michael brilliantly integrated street dance into his performance, most famously in his epic moonwalk, which bent time and collapsed space in a spasm of optical illusion that seemed to reverse motion and defy gravity. He was Einstein in a fedora. Beyoncé feminizes the geometry of flow in her surreally pliable limbs. She brings sweet antagonism to her dance discipline in a regimen of fiercely maintained and beautifully unresolved terpsichorean tensions: between formal and vernacular dance styles, between ballet and hip hop, jazz and krumping as she pivots between bust thrusts, overhead fist pumps, graceful chair choreography, head tosses, braid whips, shoulder shaking, frenetic breakdowns, tiptoe gestures, booty bumping, body rolls, hip grinding, sinuous floor crawls, double sidesteps, power stomping, spread eagles, lascivious tongue licks, runway prances, double hair flips, deep groove gyrations, arm extended airplane simulations, finger twirls and wrist twists, belly dance stomach manipulations, rubbery backbends, shimmying, air kicks, sensual undulations, twerking and booty popping, sashays, and so much more. She is Euclid in an asymmetrical leotard.

Michael's signature moonwalk dance move may have anticipated dramatic attempts later in life to reverse the inevitable march of his aging, and perhaps, vicariously, in our celebration of him, our own, in clinging desperately to the childhood that both molded and maimed him. By the time Michael gave up the ghost at 50 years old on Thursday, June 25, 2009, the same day another pop cultural icon, Farrah Fawcett, lost her battle with cancer, we may have witnessed an eerie embodiment of *The Curious Case of Benjamin Button*. In both F. Scott Fitzgerald's novel and the Oscar-nominated film version starring Brad Pitt, Benjamin Button ages in reverse: born a shriveled old man, he dies a newborn baby. As an 11-year-old prodigy, Jackson burst into the public as a miniature adult seemingly immune to small talk and child's play. His singing erupted in a volcano of sound that buried his youth beneath an implausible, irresistible sophistication. If he knew too much for his age, he may have also known too much for his own good. Jackson's art opened a window onto emotions he couldn't possibly have understood. As he got older, he repented of his precociousness and took refuge in a childlike persona that at first amused and then provoked pity and horror. He eventually flaunted a penchant for sharing his bed with children, leading to accusations of molestation. Although he was acquitted of the charges, Jackson failed to persuade skeptics in the court of public opinion. By the time he died, Michael was both loved and loathed by millions because he refused in some ways to grow up. To twist Fitzgerald's words, Jackson proved that there are no second childhoods in America.

The truth may be that both of Jackson's childhoods were imagined: the first childhood snuffed by the inspiring and imperious demands of his father, Joseph; the second childhood carved from an occasionally dangerous nostalgia for the youth he largely missed. Beyoncé had an equally energetic and engaged childhood in Houston, though in a far more stable setting than that of the working-class Jackson clan in Gary, Indiana. Beyoncé is the daughter of former sales representative Matthew and former cosmetologist Tina, Black middle-class professionals who reared Beyoncé and her younger sister, Solange, in relative comfort. Beyoncé was quite shy and had few friends, prompting her parents to sign her up for a dance class when she was seven years old. Matthew and Tina were caught by great surprise a short while later at a community show when they first witnessed Beyoncé sing and dance with a self-confidence and vibrancy they had never seen in her.

It is true that at six years old she had come home bursting with enthusiasm for the new song her first-grade teacher had taught her, unabashedly performing it for Tina while looking her squarely in the eye and brimming with vocal authority. But the kitchen was one thing, the public platform a different animal. Like Michael, Beyoncé was most alive on stage, and like him, she found her esteem and métier in performance, in the public exhibition of privately held joys through song and dance. Beyoncé entered and won many talent-show contests and beauty pageants. When she was nine, she won membership in the singing group Girls Tyme, performing with them at local competitions and national showcases, displaying her precocious talent and her prodigious work ethic while learning to compartmentalize the personal and professional, a trait that famously survived her teenage years as a star in the phenomenal girl group Destiny's Child, the successor to Girls Tyme, and into adulthood with her legendary solo career.

What Michael and Beyoncé did with their voices was noteworthy too. As a youth, Michael displayed a precocious desire to plumb the depths of his voice that harkened back to Mozart's early genius. His soaring, soulful arpeggios as he ran up and down scales like a music track star; his poignant moaning and cooing and humming that formed a golden tunnel of sound in which his notes found blissful escape; and his naked wailing and fearless vulnerability all marked his vocal magic. As Michael grew older, his voice dramatically changed; his tone radically shifted. He no longer belted out R&B tunes in a blues-drenched melisma. Instead, Jackson as a solo artist spiced his undulating tenor with sonic hiccups, parenthetical yelps, falsetto sighs, and melodic grunts, all akin to musical Tourette's. Jackson created a set of pop songs that transformed American music and evaded the racial pigeonhole. Embellishing disco, fomenting funk, and dabbling in light rock on his superb 1979 album *Off the Wall,* Jackson reached his commercial peak with 1982's *Thriller,* the bestselling album in the world of all time.

As incredible a singer as Michael was— Jackson, for instance, stylistically echoed James Brown and Jackie Wilson, and yes, Otis Redding and William Hart—Beyoncé has rivalled him with her ecstatic experimentalism that has sparked her stylistic evolution of off-kilter syncopations, rhizomes of jutting rhythms layered atop one another, and the fertile fusion of talk-rap-singing. Beyoncé can arguably be said to be the matriarch and precursor to the mumble rap style, if not its content or themes, then its slinky, esoteric phrasing and its obscuring panache that revels in elided syllables; blurred, then fused, consonants; and conjoined, or contrapuntal, ellipses. It produces a sound where meaning is destroyed and re-created, where sense is intuited, inferred, implied, and percussively insinuated rather than explicitly, or clearly, drummed into our hearing. Beyoncé's vocal prowess, now, as a mature songstress—and in her case it must be said that she *stresses* song, pressing and shaping it in the magic of her sonic embrace—matches Michael's artistic heights.

Michael's most dynamic, explosive vocal performances, on record and on stage, occurred between the ages of 8 and 21, before the prodigious weight of his transcendent singing gifts gave way to an airier sonic shimmer that he ingeniously archived in a softer and higher register of notes. When Michael came into full possession of his musical genius as auteur, he no longer possessed the range and resonance of his more brutally soulful and bluesy sound. Beyoncé, however, has grown from vocal grace to vocal grace in a steady procession from prodigy to master, mining a volatile sonic terrain that has only increased its range, depth, and power. Beyoncé's voice unleashes a cascade of notes down mountains of styles, some craggy with delightfully hostile hip hop beats that disrespect linear rhythms, others smoothed in R&B melodies and harmonies that form an archipelago of gospel grooves in her acoustic topography. Michael on stage, singing, after he reached his global fame, is no match for Beyoncé, on stage, singing, after she attained international recognition. The sheer quality of sound emanating from her durable instrument well into her thirties puts Beyoncé in a vocal stratosphere beyond Michael and her contemporaries. And when the dazzling range of her song meets the furious freedom of her body on stage, Beyoncé is in a league all her own.

But there is more to her craft than its sonic surface: Beyoncé renders pop songs as tone poems, transforming her art through stories of female aspiration, feminist resistance, and racial pride. Both Michael, starting as a child, and Beyoncé, largely as an adult, helped in their own ways to challenge and change racial and gender perceptions in America. The Jackson 5 singing group Michael formed with four of his brothers was signed to Motown Records in 1968, the year Martin Luther King, Jr., was murdered. Their string of hits starting in 1969 helped to usher in a post–civil rights version of Blackness that exploded on record with their electrifying sound and on stage with their fashionable expression of race pride. The Jackson 5 didn't have to give speeches or attend rallies to certify their authentic Blackness; the way they grew their hair and moved their bodies spelled love of their people in bold letters. Michael was a chocolate, cherubic-faced genius with an Afro halo. He and his brothers offered an image of Black masculinity that had all the style of the Black Panthers and the broad appeal of Tony the Tiger, which is why their own cartoon series—their animated artistry—helped to integrate Saturday-morning television in the early '70s. To be sure it was bubblegum, but their Blow Pops were spiked: coming only a few years after the Moynihan

Report famously concluded in 1965 that the Black family was in shambles, the Jackson 5 presented an intact unit whose image of togetherness was as revolutionary in its own way as what was happening in the courts and streets. Blacks and whites rode Michael Jackson's vocal cords into musical ecstasy and absorbed the soft racial catechism of Motown universalism without protest or resistance.

Beyoncé's Blackness has been, from the start, complicated and contested, from her time as a little girl at school when she was targeted for her light skin and hair, to her time as an adult when her racial identity and gender politics have been relentlessly questioned, both within Black life and feminist circles and far beyond. Beyoncé's Blackness has been both subliminal and subversive, both implicit and explicit, both central and incidental, nearly accidental, both taken for granted and rendered invisible, or, at the very least, innocuous. Her pop aesthetic in the white world has been read, or been interpreted, as non-Black, or nonracial, universal, transcendent. She's not a color, not a race, not a genre, not a style, not a moment in the culture's self-reckoning; she's Beyoncé, a language, a medium, an identity, a category of existence and consciousness all her own.

But her Black acts have occasionally shattered the compact of racelessness for a Black artist in America, namely, that they swear off any hint of Blackness and instead view Blackness as instrumental, that is, as critical in realizing the means to an artistic end, rather than substantive, that is, as grounding both one's approach and music—and one's themes, ideas, and identity, one's politics even—in that Blackness. Beyoncé's Black roots, her unapologetic embrace of her heritage and social protest, were displayed clearly in the video for her song "Formation." This led the legendary ensemble comedy television show *Saturday Night Live* to poke fun at the white panic the video inspired, with racial obliviousness referenced in the title of the segment: "The Day Beyoncé Turned Black."

Of course, white folk weren't the only ones worrying about Beyoncé's Blackness. Her mother, Tina Lawson, feared that the predominantly white audience at the music festival Coachella wouldn't understand all the Black cultural references, especially those associated with Black college life, that Beyoncé brilliantly explored in her Coachella sets on successive weekends in the spring of 2018. But, according to her mother, Beyoncé rebuffed her: "I have worked very hard to get to the point where I have a true voice, and at this point in my life and career, I have a responsibility to do what's best for the world and not what is most popular." This squares with Beyoncé's response to those who accused her of anti-cop sentiment during her February 2016 Super Bowl halftime performance of "Formation"—a song where she embraced Black Lives Matter and criticized police misconduct. She later insisted she admired police but drew a distinction between good and bad cops: "But let's be clear: I am against police brutality and injustice. Those are two separate things. If celebrating my roots and culture during Black History Month made anyone uncomfortable, those feelings were there long before a video and long before me. I'm proud of what we created and I'm proud to be part of a conversation that is pushing things forward in a positive way." Later, Beyoncé offered an astute diagnosis of the tragic conflation of whiteness and national identity: "It's been said that racism is so American that when we protest racism, some assume we're protesting America."

All of this concern about Beyoncé came about after she skyrocketed to fame. The more popular she became, the more she dominated global media, and art, and culture, the less Black she became in the eyes of whites here and around the world. Beyoncé overcame one of the biggest barriers of Blackness: a whiteness that fantasizes that its racial identity is neutral and that its values are universal. In such a world, even the Black object of white fantasy is transmuted into a lifestyle, a goal, an aspiration, and, finally, an icon of perfection untainted by any particular identity. Such an illusory vision can only be challenged when one is willing to contest the terms of elevation and reject the projection onto one's flesh of the apolitical ideals such a status bestows. One must be eager to embrace an identity that is seen as ineligible for cultural deification: a dirty, dark, polluted Blackness that literally rises from the dust of Western civilization to reshape the institutions of society and culture.

To paraphrase the Bible, the rejected stone of Blackness has become the cornerstone of a civilization that was suspicious of its worth and merit. Beyoncé's body is a busy intersection where dangerous collisions occur between the cranky particularity of a Blackness rooted in the skin and skill of everyday Black folk and, from another direction, a colonized and curtailed Blackness, a fetishized and toothless Blackness, a subservient and symbolic Blackness. Hers is the irreverent and irresistible Blackness of artists who come bearing the gifts of their civilizations and tribes and are willing to remake the institutions they confront through the lens of the Blackness they convey. That is how the hallowed Super Bowl stage Beyoncé commanded became an opportunity to stage an insurrectionary Blackness that jettisoned dominant meanings and substituted resistive ones. That is how Coachella went overnight from being one of the whitest showcases for artistic expression to a prominent platform for unhinged, uncontained Blackness, for metastatic Blackness, for a Blackness rooted in Black cultural styles and norms, in Black intellectual ferment, in Black college mores and folkways, and in the process got memorably rebranded as "Beychella."

Michael's image also underwent rapid transformation as he matured: his Afro got relaxed and curled, then straightened; his nose got smaller and sharper; and his skin got lighter and whiter. None of that spared Jackson racial travail. In 1980, after a *Rolling Stone* magazine publicist declined Jackson's request for a cover story, he fumed, "I've been told over and over that Black people on the cover of magazines doesn't sell copies . . . Just wait. Someday those magazines are going to be *begging* me for an interview. Maybe I'll give them one. And maybe I won't." In 1983, Jackson and his music label had to put the screws to MTV to air the video for his landmark single "Billie Jean," which opened the door for other Black artists and gave the fledgling music channel cultural cachet. Jackson essentially had to beg MTV for the opportunity to help make it rich and successful.

While Beyoncé has been widely recognized as the globe's

greatest star, she has faced her own version of artistic apartheid. Although she has garnered a gang of Grammys, she has been denied the most prestigious of those awards, including those for Record and Album of the Year. After the release of her path-breaking album *Lemonade*—a dizzying amalgam of musical genres, Black cultural allusions and references, Black iconography, carnal and spiritual desires, African female deities, serpentine phrases, trap beats, staccato cadences, and existential and institutional marital angst, all in the service of channeling rage at social inequities, especially the machinery of toxic masculinities and traitorous patriarchies, in defense of vulnerable-turned-vengeful feminisms that settle scores by naming injustices without ever having to name the men who perpetuate them, thus making it the greatest diss album of all time because in naming no guilty man it essentially names all guilty men—Beyoncé was nominated for nine Grammy awards, including in the Album, Record, and Song of the Year categories.

The Recording Academy didn't drink the *Lemonade*; the masterly album was tartly shut out of the big awards, winning only a Best Music Video Grammy and one for Best Urban Contemporary Album. In a year in which her artistic genius soared, shattered conceptual barriers, and transgressed social boundaries, Beyoncé was ghettoized and given an award to match the official musical culture's estimation of her value, as if to remind her of the narrow definitions of Blackness in which she should remain cocooned. (It was this failed recognition by the music establishment that led Kanye West to infamously protest Beyoncé's snubbing at the 2009 Video Music

Awards when Taylor Swift's "You Belong With Me" was awarded the iconic Moonman statue for Best Female Video over Beyoncé's "Single Ladies [Put a Ring on It]." West leapt on stage as Swift made her acceptance speech and broke in, saying, "Yo Taylor, I'm really happy for you. I'm a let you finish, but Beyoncé has one of the best videos of all time. One of the best videos of all time!" It was a startling gesture that occasioned great criticism of West, but it shone a harsh light on the unjust denial of recognition to Black artists.)

It is insufficient to recognize the value of Blackness in the art one consumes if you fail to recognize the value of Black art to the American enterprise. Giving Beyoncé a Grammy for Best Urban Contemporary while denying her the recognition for her American genius with the specific Grammy awards that transcend genre is to slight her Blackness and ignore her Americanness. Thus Adele, the British singer who won Album of the Year for her rousing *25*, asked, incredulously, backstage at the awards in a post-victory interview: "What the fuck does [Beyoncé] have to do to win album of the year?" Obviously be white and European.

Perhaps that fundamental recognition drove to a great degree Michael Jackson's experiments in radical self-reimagining. Michael reshaped his face in his own image, that is, the one planted in his mind by a father who teased him as a child that he was ugly. Jackson grew to believe that he was too dark and that his nose was too broad. His relentless self-mutilation through reconstructive surgery was in part a bitter projection of the self-hatred that slices the Black psyche. Although Jackson claimed to suffer from vitiligo, the disease that causes one's skin to lose pigment, he may have sought to bleach his skin to rid his face of its offending Blackness. Jackson's deconstructed face became a geography of distorted, possible faces, a fleshly region of racial ideals invaded by spooky European traits that rendered him ethnically opaque.

Beyoncé's light skin has, too, played a role in her life, in her public perception, in the politics of colorism that track her. "Sometimes in the black community, it's the lighter girls who are picked on," said Beyoncé's mother, Tina Lawson. "Of course, the opposite is often true as well, sadly—the darker girls are also picked on. It's a shame, but it's a fact of life. Beyoncé would often come home crying that the other girls were making fun of her. 'I wish I was darker,' she would say. I wanted her to embrace who she was. 'Don't wish to be anything other than what you are,' I would tell her. I know it's easy for adults to say such things, but harder for little girls to understand." Beyoncé's ethnic and racial identity has been a source of fascination on Google over the years: the search engine receives more than two thousand inquiries per month wondering "Is Beyoncé Black?," while two hundred more queries ask "Is Beyoncé full Black?," and the same number pose the question "Is Beyoncé white?" One of Beyoncé's biographers even refers to her as of mixed descent because her father is Black and her mother is "of French Creole ancestry," an observation that would render millions of Black folks of mixed descent. Beyoncé has been accused of lightening her skin. But the charge says less about Beyoncé and more about the deeply entrenched politics of colorism that dog Black culture: how lighter-skinned Black folk have enjoyed more cultural advantages than darker-skinned Blacks because of the presumption of higher intelligence, more sophisticated culture, and greater moral standing.

Despite Michael's perilous skin politics, it wasn't difficult to see the Blackness and greatness of the music he made and the broad humanity of the globally popular brand of entertainment he championed. Michael Jackson didn't get from his father the nurture, love, and unconditional affirmation he wanted in his first childhood. At times he recklessly pursued them in his failed second childhood. Still, he offered the world a glimpse of an extremely disciplined genius who was willing to share his gifts so that he could give to millions of others what he couldn't enjoy himself. That may not qualify him for martyrdom, but it does make him a remarkable, if tortured, soul who transformed his suffering into transcendent song and dance.

When Michael Jackson perished at age 50, our greatest consolation at the time was that Prince, the other Black musical genius born in the Midwest the same year as Jackson, still strode the earth in fashionable platforms. His Royal Badness's death on April 21, 2016, just as Beyoncé on April 23, 2016, poured her latest musical elixir on the world, lacked, perhaps, the synchrony of astrology and region that shaped his gentle rivalry with the King of Pop. Yet, in retrospect, we can take solace in another royal succession: as we drank the bitter dregs of a Prince leaving the scene too early, a Queen emerged in her fullest complexity yet to serve us *Lemonade* and further claim her throne as the globe's greatest entertainer. Despite their instructive differences, Prince and Beyoncé, and Michael too, remind us that the pieties of faith torch, and heal, the flesh, that musical boundaries, and those between the political and personal, can be brilliantly transgressed, and that the extravagant performances of race and gender, and sexual identity as well, often threaten the vain sovereignty of power and monoculture. Beyoncé now reigns supreme, alone, atop a kingdom of performance that she inherited from a Prince and a King but which she has made even greater.

Beyoncé's extraordinary career reflects the convergence of furious racial and gender forces as she reigns as the planet's most magnificent performer. Beyoncé has managed to command the artistic respect of her peers and the adoration of millions of fans the world over while expressing her distinct brand of feminism: the insistence that women's lives count, that their issues matter, that they be treated with respect, and that women achieve social and economic equality. Beyoncé's formidable politics of fusion—of musical styles and rhythms, of Black female deities and cultural icons, of material aspirations and spiritual desires—has reinforced her expansion of Black artistic identity by embracing queer sensibilities, amplifying progressive racial interpretations of Black suffering, and centering existence in a Black female worldview. Beyoncé is the greatest performer ever because she has absorbed and extended the best traits and wisest lessons of Michael Jackson in her ever-evolving, tirelessly shapeshifting hunger for excellence. Whether singing, dancing, rapping, making videos or documentaries, or using her art to

protest, rally, signify, edify, and, above all, to entertain, Beyoncé
is an outsize genius whose quest for greatness has blazed a path
that no one before her has traveled and, undoubtedly, few, if any,
after her can successfully pursue.

Beyoncé the Brave

―――◆―――

RESHMA SAUJANI

I grew up in Schaumburg, Illinois, in the 1980s. Back then, I hated the color of my skin. I wished that my mom wouldn't wear a sari in the local Kmart. I was embarrassed when my friends came over and my house smelled like Indian food. I wanted so badly to just look like everyone else, to blend in. I wished my parents had given me a "more American name." I prayed every day that I wouldn't wake up to a house that was egged or TPed because the people in it—my family—didn't look like everyone else.

Back then, I didn't really know who I was. Every day was another day trying to assimilate, to make myself look like, talk like, act like the others. Then, on the last day of eighth grade, something changed. Another classmate called me something derogatory, and for the first time (and last time ever) I got into a physical fight after school. I was beat up pretty badly, but I was proud to rock that black eye. I was proud that I didn't walk away from a fight.

That was the day I started connecting more with my Indian identity, seeking out people who looked like me. I was reborn to fight for inclusivity and for people who are the most vulnerable. That was when I started feeling proud of myself.

No matter how powerful Beyoncé has become, no matter how rich she's become, she's never let anybody forget where she comes from or who she is. For me, that's being a true role model.

I've met Beyoncé twice: once at an event for Michelle Obama at an Italian restaurant in the West Village, and once at the Justice for Trayvon rally in 2013. At the rally, I was in a prayer circle with about a dozen people backstage—including Beyoncé and Jay-Z. It was a moment I'll never forget. We were just a group of parents, children, hurting and healing in community. Beyoncé didn't show up as Beyoncé, as Queen Bey—she showed up as a mother and—more specifically—a Black mother. She and Jay-Z showed up to the rally out of love, love for the lives of young boys like Trayvon who were, and still are, being murdered in our streets.

It's important for all of us to show up, for justice, for our young people, for ourselves and as ourselves.

Growing up, I didn't have South Asian role models. Now, every week, I'll get an email from a young Indian girl and I'm the subject of her book report or she's dressing up like me for Women's History Month. Because of them, I never deny who I am. I show up as my whole self. I talk about where I came from and about my refugee parents. I talk about my name being Reshma, and how I refused to change it when I ran for political office in 2010.

Like Beyoncé, the more my platform expands, the more I will talk about who I am and where I come from. I want more brown girls to see themselves in my journey, and to see themselves in the field of technology.

Culture has done a good job telling girls and women, especially those who aren't white, that they belong in certain places and not in others. They should be successful, but not too successful. They should only work in certain fields, and not others. In my line of work, I see every day the barriers that girls face in the boys' club of computer science.

Our girls still grow up with dolls that say "I hate math, let's go shopping instead." They can buy shirts that say, "I'm allergic to algebra." They can turn on the TV, and see boys and men playing the part of coders and scientists and mathematicians. If Hollywood said, "It is our commitment to have more *Hidden Figures*, more Katherine Johnsons, to tell more of these stories and to put them in front of girls," then this problem could be solved in a generation.

I have hope things will get better. We've already seen so much progress and energy around women's empowerment. For me and a lot of other girls and women, Beyoncé has played a key role in that progress.

She has always pushed me to extend my boundaries as a leader and as a woman. When I was a student at Yale we had a crew of eight women, mostly women of color, who would listen to "Survivor" and her other anthems of vulnerability and strength on repeat. Sixteen years later, I still listen to her music when I'm revving up for a speech and I want to feel powerful.

And sometimes I need to feel powerful even if I'm not standing onstage.

I have a condition where I suffer from recurrent miscarriages. There was a very dark period in my life between 2012 and 2014 when I suffered from several of them. It seemed as if every time my husband and I would go to the hospital for a checkup at the beginning of a pregnancy, it would end terribly.

We'd enter the exam room, impatient to see the sonogram, anxious to hear a heartbeat that inevitably was no longer there. The fourth time I got pregnant, it was more of the same: going to appointments and sitting in cold exam rooms for news. Except this time the soundtrack to that journey was Beyoncé's "XO." There's a line in it about seeing someone through the darkness. That spoke to my heart. I envisioned seeing my child and loving him so much that I would be with him one day through this darkness. That song gave me strength and hope. It got me through my darkness.

There's still so much shame around miscarriage and also this pressure to be quiet and pretend everything is okay. I stayed quiet for a long time. But now I talk about my journey to becoming a mother—and the trouble I had having children—all the time. I talk about my miscarriages, about complications with pregnancy. I do this because no one, no mother, should ever feel alone.

When Beyoncé opened up in her documentary about having her miscarriage, and then more recently in *Vogue* about her pregnancy with the twins—her emergency C-section, the grueling recovery, her changing body—that meant so much to me and to so many women I know.

That's what we want from people we admire: we want authenticity. We want flaws, we want to know that they—like us—have faced challenges, survived, and thrived.

Beyoncé's authenticity and vulnerability are what makes her simultaneously relatable and iconic.

I talk a lot about the importance of bravery in this culture of perfection—about how girls are raised to be perfect, discouraged from failing, from being brave. I started being brave when I started embracing my Indian identity, then again when I ran for political office twice and lost each time, and then again when I so badly wanted a child but had to face disappointment over and over and over again. Every time I chose bravery, my world didn't end. Every time, even when it felt impossible, I was able to get up and keep going. Every time, I came out stronger.

Beyoncé inspired that bravery in me then, and still does now. She is the epitome of what it means to be a brave, not perfect, woman. And we all love her for it.

Living into the *Lemonade*:

Redefining Black Women's

Spirituality in the Age of Beyoncé

———•———

CANDICE BENBOW

She is an international superstar, yes, but many forget that Beyoncé is also a Southern church girl steeped in Black church aesthetic and traditions. While her music and iconic status boast an unapologetic sexuality, she has not detoured from the instructions church girls have been given in her personal life. Marrying Jay before birthing Blue, Beyoncé followed the trajectory that the church assured would result in uninterrupted bliss and happiness. If there is anything Black Southern girls know, it's that nothing is more important than obedience to God. It is the foundation for a successful life. But what happens when all of your success contradicts everything the church taught us? For the church, Beyoncé is indeed a complicated figure. On one hand, she got married and then started a family, as all good Christian girls are instructed. On the other hand, as a single woman, she embodied a body politic that we were told wouldn't yield her that husband and family in the first place. What do you do with women like Beyoncé? What do women like Beyoncé do with themselves?

Beyoncé's solo career was the soundtrack of our twenties. We knew her. We grew up with her. She was the pretty girl in high school, the captain of the dance squad. All the boys loved her. None of the girls wanted to, but her kindness surpassed her beauty and she was just too nice to hate. But even though we loved her, one glimpse at her videos and you knew your mother would have nipped your friendship in the bud real quick. While her Southern roots of faith and family were always clear, Bey was just a different kind of church girl—one much freer than any of us were ever taught God wanted us to be.

Maybe that's why she needed Sasha Fierce. For years, we understood Beyoncé's dominating, sultry, and sexual alter ego as the antithesis to her Southern, demure, girl-next-door disposition. Everyone who thought Beyoncé was too grown and too sexual was given a sufficient explanation: Sasha only existed for the stage. People could rest easy knowing that this young woman, who would one day become the greatest living entertainer, was good and wholesome in her everyday life. Having and owning that kind of sexual power and agency, as a Black woman, will never be met with overwhelming praise. Whether people are actively religious or not, the assertions made about

Black female sexuality have long been rooted in theological beliefs that see Black women's bodies as tools for others to exploit and never for Black women themselves to enjoy. We grew up on a steady diet of sermons where scripture was often misconstrued to suggest that none of the women that we admire in the Bible possess any sexual agency. We watched as pastors continually scolded single mothers from the pulpit as if they got pregnant by themselves. We Southern girls knew better than to believe a healthy sexual identity was what God wanted for us. But, as the generation raised equally by the Black church and by hip hop, these messages just don't hold up under the weight of scrutiny and common sense.

Still, we wanted to be good girls navigating what we "knew" to be right and what we felt. During her Destiny's Child days and at the beginning of her solo career, Bey helped us with that journey. On the DC albums, we always got that one obligatory gospel song. My friends and I called it the "Jesus track." And on Bey's first solo projects, if the songs weren't explicitly gospel, they were so church adjacent that they could be sung during a Sunday service by the youth choir. These songs all worked to prove that, though Beyoncé was a young woman owning her sexual prowess, she hadn't strayed too far from her Christian roots. Those inside Southern Black church culture knew such a declaration was important. As Southern church girls, we were taught to steer clear of suggestive and explicit music. We were never to sing or perform anything that would cause our brothers to be tempted to sin. Good girls just didn't do that. We were supposed to be poised and chaste and, as a church girl, Beyoncé knew this. And yet, we consistently saw her popping and dropping, giving us hit after hit to help us perfect our twerk and whine. But, she didn't leave us without penance. If the rest of the album made us sin on Saturday night, we could count on at least one song we could sing as we pulled into the church parking lot on Sunday morning.

Growing up in St. John's United Methodist Church in North-west Houston, Beyoncé's theological formation was more pro-gressive than most. Known for fostering a gospel of inclusivity and acceptance, Beyoncé's church offered different messages about faith and sexuality—messages that would undoubt-edly shape her personal relationship with God and her profes-sional career. But despite her progressive theological formation, Beyoncé could not escape the bifurcation of Black women's spiritual and sexual identity. We can't know how she dealt with the struggle internally. However, as church girls, many of us understood those "Jesus tracks" and Sasha Fierce's exis-tence as Bey's attempts to navigate the liminal space of fully owning her budding pop icon status and proving that she was still the same sweet girl from Houston. We try so hard to please people and much of Beyoncé's likability came from her ability to separate her sensuality from her spirit. Yes—on stage, she had a wanton sexuality, but, in real life, she was a good Southern girl raised on Jesus and sweet tea. Living two lives can become too much for anyone. So, when Beyoncé told us Sasha Fierce died in 2010, we understood it. There was a synergy Bey longed for that couldn't be found in a space where she had to pick and choose who she would be and when she would be her.

If Sasha went on to glory in 2010, we saw the impact of her passing in 2011 with the release of *IV*. Quite possibly the most definitive album of her career, *IV* introduced us to a Beyoncé who was taking control of her career. From her image to her sound, everything would be solely her design. And while that album would arguably lay the foundation of Beyoncé's ascension into that otherworldly status of icons where few reside, it was the surprise self-titled album that made it clear we would never see Sasha Fierce again. Beyoncé somehow secretly recorded and filmed visuals for an entire album that oozed sex, celebrated love, and honored the feminine power of the divine in a way that changed music and young Black womanhood forever. We'd begun to see glimpses of this newfound self-determination since the birth of Blue Ivy, but *Beyoncé* took things to an unexpected level. To many, it seemed she had something to prove. Maybe she did. To others, it seemed she was tired of playing by the rules. It was as if Beyoncé was telling everybody that she could be all of these things within herself—erotic, maternal, political, spiritual—and, if anyone had a problem with it, it was theirs and not hers.

Just as *IV*'s pronouncement of freedom created space for *Beyoncé*'s total liberation, it all made way for the holy magic that is *Lemonade*. Beyoncé shares that the pain of betrayal has infiltrated her home and, to cope, she turns to what she knows best: God and the church. She finds herself at the altar, pleading for God to make a way—a place she has seen her own mother before. Beyoncé follows the instructions she's been given to endure these tough times as a dutiful Christian woman:

> *Fasted for sixty days . . . confessed my sins and was baptized in a river . . .*

But something remains insufficient; the praying and the fasting are unable to keep her husband faithful. The pleas for divine intervention are unable to keep her from spiraling. Bey's next movements are destructive, not only to the people around her but also to herself. She has invested so much of herself in a love that has harmed her and she reacts accordingly. In church, we're taught to give it to God; rage can't exist in the heart of a woman who is fully committed to her faith. In *Lemonade*, Beyoncé rejects that. It is possible to deeply love God and have a strong, human reaction to the pain caused by those we trust. There is a space for us to live into the fullness of our humanity. We have watched women in our families and congregations deny their emotions in hopes to please a God who only desires authenticity. Beyoncé's generation of church girls will offer their God and the world exactly that, making our own *Lemonade* in ways that will contradict much of what we've been taught.

Because of traditional Christianity's controversial and contradictory messages of Black womanhood and sexuality, I truly believe it's impossible for Black women's spirituality to experience fullness solely in the mainstream church. *Lemonade* reflects the harmony many Black women have found once they accepted this. In the same work, Beyoncé lifted the Christian God and the Oshun, illustrating how she stands in a long tradition of Black women who have crafted their own spiritual freedom. Those mothers and sages live by their own rules and consistently encourage us to do the same. We see the fruit of their wisdom not just in Beyoncé's art but in her life. If she left it up to the Beyhive and courts of public opinion, she would have ended her marriage. If she left it up to the church, she would have silently endured her husband's infidelity and internalized his failings as her own. Instead, she honored her own humanity by requiring accountability and growth. For those who wanted her to leave, Beyoncé showed that it is possible to stay and fight for something beautiful. For those who wanted her to act as if nothing happened, Mrs. Knowles-Carter reminded her husband of her power and made him work for it. But more than anything, the icon proved that the death of her Sasha Fierce alter ego and the independence that began in the *IV* album weren't publicity stunts. She is different. She is always who she wants to be and is encouraging us to become the same.

After watching *Lemonade*, many Black women became thirsty for what would allow them to remain in such an informed space of transparency. While live tweeting the HBO premiere, many of us were lifted by the Black feminist and womanist themes that were weaved throughout the film. Sis channeled Toni, Alice, Maya, Zora, and all of the greats. She gave us *Daughters of the Dust, The Color Purple,* and *Eve's Bayou* vibes. It was absolutely glorious and Black women wanted more. With the contributions of over 70 Black women, I created the *Lemonade* Syllabus as a free, downloadable resource that speaks to Black womanhood in its historical and contemporary manifestations. *Lemonade* unleashed emotions Black women had long suppressed or refused to acknowledge and we needed to address them. I know it did for me. Navigating the recent loss of my mother and questioning the future of a relationship I wanted to last, I leaned into everything I was feeling—anger, confusion, frustration, hope—and created the Syllabus. It opened up the space for me to be honest about my pain, think a new way forward, and create my own healing and wholeness. I'm thankful that it did the same for other women, too. Across the country, Black women started *Lemonade* Syllabus book clubs to work through the Syllabus in its entirety. Universities have created *Lemonade* Syllabus courses that will look at the Syllabus as a Black feminist work along with *Lemonade* and Beyoncé's overall cultural impact. And there have been *Lemonade* Syllabus "stands" at public libraries where I've also had the opportunity to discuss the global importance of Black feminist and womanist literature.

Great art is inspirational and transformative. We are not in a post-*Lemonade* moment. More aptly, we are living into it. If we are to apply the lessons of *Lemonade* fully, we must first move away from the spaces that have harmed us. A misguided critique of *Lemonade* is that Bey's reconciliation with Jay is encouragement to remain in abusive relationships. It is quite the opposite; we are actually being encouraged to leave places that refuse accountability and do not intend to love us well. This is not limited to Black women's personal relationships. Black women are navigating professional and spiritual relationships that are death dealing and, if we need it, *Lemonade* is giving us permission to leave. And our response to *Lemonade* calls us to move toward the *Lemonade* itself. It requires that Black women live into their flourishing. Black women's living in America is hard; yet that is not the totality of the story. Black women have been able to thrive in the face of death and isolation. Living into the *Lemonade* calls us to focus on the thriving more than the circumstances that oppose it. When Black women live into the *Lemonade*, they are choosing a joy that refuses to be diminished by the violence that will continue to persist against them. It is the joy of Grandma's kitchen table where she will feed your malnourished body and wounded spirit. It is the joy of Black hair salons where Black women provide each other temporary refuge from the wages of Black life in America. It is the joy of every Beyoncé world tour where Black women describe their experience as spiritual, saying she took them to church. Black women have always found ways to live into the *Lemonade*, and if sisters will continue to flourish, this must become our permanent posture.

We all have fought our way back from some very painful experiences and we deserve to celebrate that. Those lemons, tart as they may be, are not the end of the story. We made something despite of them; we made a life—a sweet one. Here's to enjoying every sip.

Beyoncé's Radical Ways

————◆————

CARMEN PEREZ

W*hen it comes* to political identity, Beyoncé is a sophisticated, underappreciated power. She has been able to bring radicalism onto a stage in an unprecedented way given her influence and reach. We need agents of change to march and protest, but we also need people to take the movement to the mainstream and that's what she's done time and again. She is using her platform to heighten awareness of important social causes like police brutality and feminism.

My mentor, Harry Belafonte, Mr. B, often talks about *his* mentor: the artist and political activist Paul Robeson. He was the first Black person Mr. B saw take a stage. And when Mr. Belafonte was beginning in his career, Paul Robeson came to see him to talk about breaking racial barriers in the arts. Mr. B says, "For me, Mr. Robeson was the sparrow. He was an artist who made those of us in the arts understand the depth of that calling, when he said, 'Artists are the gatekeepers of truth. We are civilization's radical voice.' Never in the history of black America has there been such a harvest of truly gifted and powerfully celebrated artists. Yet, our nation hungers for their radical song. In the field of sports, our presence dominates. In the landscape of corporate power, we have more African-American presence as captains and leaders of industry than we've ever known. Yet we suffer still from abject poverty and moral malnutrition."

It was family tragedy that became fuel for my activism. My sister Patricia, only two years older than me, was killed. She was buried on my seventeenth birthday. I played basketball growing up, so instead of mourning her loss I took it out on the court. I went away to college; studied psychology; got involved with theater. I needed a "day job" so I also started working with young people who were incarcerated or formerly incarcerated, trying to help them find their voice. I created several programs offering alternatives to incarceration and, through an organization called Barrios Unidos, I started organizing cultural and spiritual ceremonies and programs: Juneteenth, Cinco de Mayo, and pow wows inside the Deuel Vocational Institution, also known as Tracy prison, for men who were facing life sentences. Through doing this work, I met my mentor, Nane Alejandrez, who ultimately introduced me to Mr. Belafonte.

I was brought in as one of the mentees in a larger conversation to look at abolishing child incarceration as a moral imperative. It was while I was participating in those meetings that I got to meet Mr. Belafonte. He was building a movement using Kingian nonviolence, which is the ideology of Dr. King, as the foundation for civic engagement, political action, and for shifting the narrative when it came to youth incarceration. And he asked me to join him. I initially came onboard as national organizing director to help build the organization, The Gathering for Justice. I became the executive director in 2010, and since then I've started two state-based task forces, Justice League NYC and now Justice League CA, which coordinate advocacy around critical legislative changes to end mass incarceration. Between The Gathering for Justice, which is Mr. Belafonte's legacy, and Justice League, we are able to connect influencers to the issues that impact the lives, particularly, of Black and brown people when it comes to incarceration, policing, and women's rights. The 2017 Women's March on Washington was also connected to Mr. B's legacy in a special way, since The Gathering for Justice immediately became an incubator for the initial idea. I was one of the four national co-chairs and Mr. Belafonte was named honorary chair out of respect for his role in the 1964 March on Washington and his immense legacy in movement building throughout his life.

Beyoncé has long incorporated political messaging into her art and follows through with concrete activism. For her, the personal truly is political. She identifies as a feminist and exemplifies Black excellence; she has hired this extraordinary team—from the stage to the office—of mostly women of color, creating both economic and creative opportunity for marginalized people. Her philanthropic activism is intentionally positioned to uplift all women—but Black women particularly.

Right now we're trying to create the fifth wave of feminism, which Beyoncé embodies. She takes us back to the true essence of intersectional feminism, which is grounded in radical black feminism and centers the needs of marginalized communities. She models a type of feminism that says, I can both challenge and uplift the men in my community. Beyoncé is subtle and eloquent: inclusive, intentional, and intersectional, and in that way, she models new ways of being for women like myself who identify as feminists.

Lemonade was such a potent mix of activism, power, and vulnerability, all served in ferocious doses. There were so many of us who could relate because of the pain, outrage, and resilience she conveyed. I remember playing that album while we were organizing "A Day without a Woman," which was a solidarity action on International Women's Day 2017, and that music made us feel inspired and connected to our identity as feminists, as women, as activists. For me, liberation music is art that touches and uplifts our different and intersecting identities.

Beyoncé also shows up in the mainstream spaces where we still need to have these courageous conversations. She enters the homes of many Americans who have never had a conversation about Black Lives Matter, who have never had a conversation about feminism. For instance, she used the Super Bowl as her opportunity to bring the issue of police brutality onto that mainstream stage. Think about it: even with the work I do, those are my brothers still watching the Super Bowl—they're not activists, they're not engaged in conversations on feminist theory, they're not engaged in the Black liberation movement. What Beyoncé is doing is key, relevant, and necessary, bringing a very different conversation to families that might not have been having conversations about the movement.

At the 2013 NAACP Image Awards, Mr. B gave a tremendous speech on gun control. He talked about the blood of Black children flowing through the streets of America. He called out the church, politicians, and the community to act. He said, in part:

> The group that is most devastated by America's obsession with the gun is African Americans. Although making comparisons can be dangerous, there are times when they must be noted. America has the largest prison population in the world, and of the over two million men, women and children who make up the incarcerated, the overwhelming majority of them are black. African Americans are the most unemployed, the most caught in the unjust systems of justice. And in the gun game, they are the most hunted. The rivers of blood that wash the streets of our nation flow mostly from the bodies of our black children. Yet, as the great debate emerges on the question of the gun, white America discusses the constitutional issues of ownership, while no one speaks to the consequences of our racial carnage. Where is the outraged voice of black America? Where? And why are we mute? Where are our leaders? Where are our legislators? Where is the church?

Immediately after Mr. B's speech, Jamie Foxx was supposed to receive an award. But he literally could not speak after Mr. Belafonte had spoken, so powerful was the effect of this speech on him. Jamie Foxx, Talib Kweli, Common, John Legend, and others reached out to Mr. B after his speech for mentorship and guidance on how to craft a creative life that is more deeply and effectively grounded in activism. Mr. B also spoke with Jesse Williams and Dave Chappelle and many other influencers who are constantly reaching out. This has reignited the type of relationships that were nourished during the Civil Rights movement, and the Gathering for Justice has built a body of work based on that legacy of building relationships between artists and movement builders.

This moment that we are in was also ushered in by a unique confluence of technology and the rise of social media as the tool of concerned and committed citizens. We have information at the tips of our fingers through social media and video cameras built into all our phones; and so, in the killings of unarmed black and brown people by police, each individual story cannot be sidelined or justified by the powers that be as in the past. I think we saw that with Oscar Grant, but it became very different when it happened to Trayvon Martin and then increasingly different when it happened to Michael Brown in Ferguson. There was this sense of urgency, and social media played a huge role in us being able to provide information and to share the stories of people on the ground who were narrating events. Police brutality has long been part of our narrative as people of color in this country. The difference now is that with the technological tools of smartphones and social media, we are able to get around media gatekeepers and publicly bear witness to the crimes that are committed.

When Mr. Belafonte called out Jay-Z and Beyoncé for not being socially responsible as celebrities with wealth and power, the comment was taken completely out of context. He did not mean to minimize their work, but he argued that we had not seen many artists of their stature take a visible position when it came to any of these issues. They may have been donating to organizations on a quiet, private trajectory. But we've seen that so many PR people use the language of privacy, when what they really mean is they don't want their clients to take the risk of a visible, political position.

There was an opportunity for the three to reconcile when Nelson Mandela died. At that point, Jay-Z's mother said, "You need to make things right with this man," because Jay-Z had released an album with a song that kind of presents Mr. B in a very negative light. So I got a call from a woman named dream hampton, who works closely with Jay-Z, as well as from Jasiri X, and they said "Hey, is there any way you could get a message to Mr. B?" And so Mr. B and Jay-Z met and talked privately, and to this day they still have conversations. They've been able to build a deep respect and a rapport. Because of that relationship, The Gathering for Justice was able to work with Roc Nation and other groups when Meek Mill was wrongfully incarcerated, ultimately leading to his release.

In our organization, we connect the stars to the people who are on the ground. For instance, T.I. might text me to inquire about organizations that are working on the frontlines when an incident occurs in a specific community. Ebro Darden, host of Hot 97's morning show, has used his platform to speak out on the issues and now serves on the board of directors for The Gathering for Justice. When the Dream Defenders led a month-long sit-in at the Florida state house after the acquittal of George Zimmerman in 2013, Mr. Belafonte and myself went down there and we put Q-Tip, David Banner, Talib Kweli, and others on a call with the Dream Defenders executive director, so they were able to support the efforts that were happening on the ground. Recently, I worked with Colin Kaepernick to connect him to trainers for his Know Your Rights camps for young people.

Sometimes people aren't willing to take a visible political stance because it can backfire. Colin Kaepernick is being blacklisted for his political stance. I have such a deep respect for his courage to do the right thing despite the backlash. Audre Lorde once wrote, "When we speak we are afraid our words will not be heard or welcomed. But when we are silent, we are still afraid. So it is better to speak."

Beyoncé has been an inspiration because she speaks out, strategically using her own stage, her own platform, to amplify the messages of Black liberation and Black excellence. You have to watch the cultural moments that are happening concurrently: there is this tremendous sense of pride over having Bey in Coachella and playing the Black National Anthem. The inspiration that she has provided for so many young women of color is really immeasurable.

You need to have that song in your head, you need to be assured and confident in your humanity when, in that same week, you are also seeing Chikesia Clemons being violently assaulted and dragged out of Waffle House. Beyoncé needs to continue to do what she does so well because it makes a difference. Even as Black lives are being disvalued, she's saying Black lives are excellent. That Black girls are magic, strong and beautiful. Reaffirming that they come from kings and queens. We all need to remember that.

I think Beyoncé probably has always been political, except people did not notice early on. They didn't notice because she has made music that is very mainstream and you have to listen deeply in order to understand that there's a radicalism in her authenticity and these indie windows of subliminal messages. She is very discreet. Even her relationship with Jay in the beginning was very private. But she has been able to transition into politics unexpectedly. The difference between her and other artists is that she's been very strategic about where her platform has been used, how it's been used, what she's messaging.

It takes a certain kind of power to speak your mind and to speak specifically to people of color and women when you're in the public eye. Mr. Belafonte has lived long enough, and been through enough, that he has a deep historical analysis and he is able to voice a very unique perspective on the current political climate. That's why he's still relevant, why he's such a great advisor and mentor to so many, even at 91 years old. What I love about Beyoncé is the way in which she's been very strategic about her activism—she's not called a liberal, yet look at how radical her imagery and her lyrics can be. I can't wait to witness her growth and evolution by the time she reaches Mr. B's age.

Finding *La Reina* in Queen Bey

———•———

ISABEL GONZÁLEZ WHITAKER

It wasn't until the third time that I met Beyoncé that she showed me her superpower.

The first two times, in the late nineties, I just said hello at record industry meet and greets, where Destiny's Child was working hard to get fans to say their names. The third and fourth times were a decade later, in 2008 and 2011, by which time Beyoncé had reached certified solo status, as an artist and in name, and I interviewed her for cover stories for *InStyle* magazine, where I worked as an editor.

The first time I sat down with her, I was nervous and new to my job, as well as emotionally fragile, having lost my mother a few weeks prior. Beyoncé was my first true superstar interview. I remember exactly what I wore because I gave it tons of thought, as you do when you are going to meet an artist you have long admired. But I was also there to get a job done, so I chose a boxy Maria Cornejo black top paired with a black high-waist wool gabardine Stella McCartney skirt, Lucite wedge heels from United Nude, and one of my mom's chunky necklaces for good luck. My boss told me I looked chic, which was what I was aiming for. Beyoncé complimented my shoes, which is why I'm sitting here now wondering why I ever got rid of them.

I'm sure she could tell I was nervous, though I tried my best to project confidence and stay focused, even as my mind wandered to my mother and how I wished I could tell her how nice Beyoncé was to me, how pretty she was, and to tell her what Beyoncé wore (a green jumpsuit by YSL, my mother's favorite designer).

Near the end of our allotted hour, sitting next to her on a black leather couch in the industrial photo studio, I glanced at my list of unasked questions and knew I wasn't going to have time to get to them. I don't think I appeared flustered, but she picked up on my anxiety nonetheless. When a handler came in to end the interview, Beyoncé told her that we were fine and to give us more time. "Go ahead," she told me: "Ask what you need to." I exhaled and thanked her.

The last question of the interview was about her desire to eventually play a superhero in a movie. "What would be your superpower if you could have one in real life?" I asked. "The power to disappear and just watch people," she replied. "The older I get, I can see what people are going to do—it's not like I'm psychic, I just have a good read on people. It's really what I do. I walk into a room and I read people." On that day, I very much appreciated her superpower.

Each time I've met her she's been warm but with interpersonal boundaries that convey the hard-working professional she is: firm handshakes, sustained eye contact, focus and attention to the questions. She means business but she's kind, smiles a lot, and is quick to laugh at herself. What struck me the most though was how supportive she was of me, and it's why I know her sense of sisterhood is real, that she truly is a woman's woman.

That interview is also when I first learned that her best friend is Cuban, like me, and about her love of Latin culture and food. It struck me because as a Latina I've always been drawn to her look. I was taught from a young age to notice and admire women who dress well, who wear makeup and high heels and show feminine silhouettes—signifiers I've always identified as specific to the Latin world I grew up in. I learned from my grandmothers, great aunts, mother, sister, and their friends that to look polished and put together meant that you were healthy and life was good. The Latin fashion culture, especially Caribbean influenced, loves flair with bold colors, prints, and ruffles. It's a feminine aesthetic that's sexy, with body-conforming cuts that accentuate curves (and remember, curves are a good thing). It's lipstick, accessories, and leg-elongating stilettos. In that first interview, Beyoncé told me how she didn't feel dressed without big earrings, she shared her love of platform heels, and she talked about how her mother—who hails from a Creole family from Caribbean-influenced southern Louisiana and grew up on the Gulf in Galveston, Texas—made sure she and her sister Solange always had their blush or lip gloss with them in their purses. It doesn't get more Latin than loyalty to lip gloss and a mother's ire at stepping out of the house undone. "When you look at beauty and the Southern black girl it can be indistinguishable from beauty as presented in Dominican culture or Cuban culture," says Africana Studies expert Zandria Robinson. "There's a shared focus on beauty, elegance, femininity and the presentation of the self."

This specific brand of beauty and femininity is of course also on display in Beyoncé's album artwork, videos, and social media accounts, and there has been speculation about her visual embrace of the West African deities that influence and define the spiritual aspects of the Latin Caribbean region from Santería in Cuba to Candomblé in Brazil. When she wears head-to-toe yellow (a silk-tiered ruffled Roberto Cavalli marigold gown in *Lemonade*'s "Hold Up" video) or ornate gold (a gold crown and lace dress by Peter Dundas at the 2017 Grammys), could that be referencing Oshun, the Yoruba deity of sexuality, fertility, and beauty? Other images and outfits conjure Yemaya, a powerful water deity. "The religious symbols that she incorporates into her work draw a line across the Africa diaspora," says Andrea Gompf, editor in chief of the Latinx news and entertainment website Remezcla. "The references to the Yoruba deities surface the connectedness of African Americans and Latin Americans."

Beyond her appearance, there's also Beyoncé's decades-long embrace of Latin music: With Destiny's Child she sang with Spanish crooner and global superstar Alejandro Sanz on the Latin Grammys in 2002; in 2006, she dropped an EP of Spanish covers from *B'Day*, including "Amor Gitano" with famed Mexican singer Alejandro Fernández, which was used as the theme song for a beloved Zorro-themed telenovela; in 2008, she released a Spanish version of "If I Were a Boy." But last year saw her biggest Spanish-language hit, a remix of Colombian reggaeton star J. Balvin and French DJ and producer Willy William's global dance hit *"Mi Gente."* It sat on the Billboard Hot 100 for 30 weeks, peaking at number three. She donated proceeds from the song to hurricane relief efforts in Puerto Rico, Mexico, and the Caribbean, areas that had been hard hit by Hurricanes Irma and Maria.

As a gangly Cuban teenager growing up in Atlanta in the 1980s, my musical taste was informed by the videos I'd watch after school on MTV—Whitney, Madonna, Michael—and my parents' vinyl collection. Their taste was varied but cool, from Willie to Aretha, from Stevie to Billy, and of course Gloria and Celia, the dual patron saints of Cuban music. Even though my parents were immigrants from the island, Latin music wasn't the exclusive soundtrack of their adult lives in Atlanta, and it wasn't my soundtrack growing up as one of the few Latin kids in my school.

Despite the visceral pull of the horn-driven rhythms, tropical-inflected Latin music didn't resonate for me. Maybe it's because I wasn't a good salsa dancer like my parents and siblings, or maybe it was because Latin songs—even the popular ones at the time from Miami Sound Machine—weren't played at the skating rink or appreciated by my classmates. But even when kids poked fun at Gerardo's *"Rico Suave,"* I was proud of its testimony to the fact that our world existed within pop culture, even if it was shunted over toward the margins.

I didn't develop a deeper sense of pride and faithful listening until my twenties, when I'd visit my brother, who by then was living in South Beach. Music in Miami is everywhere—blasted from cars and boats during the day and blaring at night from clubs, where we'd go to dance to electronic, house, and Latin music. Quieter moments at my brother's home were spent exploring his record collection, learning about Benny Moré and La Lupe. But that was Miami in the midnineties, when Gianni Versace was hosting lavish parties at his Ocean Drive mansion, introducing the world to Albita. I may have started to get hip to the history, influence, and richness of Latin music, but outside of Miami and with the exception of pockets of New York, Texas, and California, the rest of the country was still a few years away from accepting it as the hot sound.

That's one of the reasons why I'm so happy that as I write this, the summer of 2018, history is being made: Dominican American stripper-cum–reality star–cum urban artist Cardi B, nee Belcalis Almánzar, has become the first female rapper with two number ones on the Billboard Hot 100. Her first, 2017's Louboutin-loving "Bodak Yellow (Money Moves)," peaked in October of that year, and now she's charting with "I Like It," an urban take on "I Like It Like That," the seminal Nuyorican hit of the late 1960s by Pete Rodriguez. And while Cardi isn't breaking records for being a Latina appearing at the top of the world's most important music consumption chart (Jennifer Lopez did it four times, that last time with 2003's "All I Have"), it's a significant achievement on a chart that more often features non-Latinos in the top slots and songs in English. "I Like It" is mostly sung in Spanish, thanks to features by Puerto Rican trap artist Bad Bunny and Colombia's J. Balvin.

It gives both Balvin and Bunny their first number ones,

though Balvin came close last year with the Beyoncé remix of *"Mi Gente."* The song was actually already surging before Beyoncé—and daughter Blue, who contributes four words to the track—jumped in. But her participation, in Spanish no less, took it higher on the charts and gave it the ultimate seal of tastemaker approval. Its popularity was also aided by recent audience receptivity to Latin music's crossover appeal: in 2014, Enrique Iglesias, Descemer Bueno, and Gente de Zona broke records with their ubiquitous urban pop Spanish-language song "Bailando" and in 2017, Luis Fonsi, Daddy Yankee, and Justin Bieber broke even more records with "Despacito," including being the first song ever to get five billion views on YouTube.

Beyoncé's fans, Latin or not, loved it and showed their support, especially on Twitter, where they playfully conjugated her name into a tutorial on Spanish grammar.

@cultA_KIAish
Beyoncó
Beyoncés
Beyoncé
Beyoncémos
Beyoncéis
Beyoncéin
9:41pm Sep 28, 2017

"To have someone like Beyoncé, with her huge global stature, recognize and acknowledge Latino artists and pay her respect is very meaningful to the artists and to Latino fans," says Gompf. "We are living in a moment right now where artists with huge mainstream visibility are embracing our language and our culture—not the other way around." And if anyone wants to question her motives they need only look at the 2002 performance on the Latin Grammys. "She prioritized us from the beginning of her career and we haven't forgotten," says Gompf.

It's no coincidence that the chairman and CEO of Sony Music at the time, Tommy Mottola, who signed Destiny's Child in 1996, had a hand in the Latin Grammy performance, an awards show he helped CBS launch in 2000. Mottola grew up in the Bronx, where "Tito Puente was as much a part of the musical fabric as pop and rock 'n roll," he says. As the head of Sony he ushered in a Latin wave in the late nineties by signing and pushing out Shakira, Ricky Martin, Jennifer Lopez, Marc Anthony, and Gloria Estefan. He was also the architect of the Latin Explosion in 1999 when Latin artists like Ricky Martin and Jennifer Lopez all sat in the top ten of Billboard's Hot 100 with Latin-tinged English-language songs. While his Latin artists were having success in English, Mottola encouraged his roster, from Mariah Carey to Celine Dion to Jennifer Lopez, to record in Spanish. "The Latin demographic loved those stars so it was a simple equation: give them the songs they loved in English but also in Spanish," he says. As for Beyoncé, "she's always been a trendsetter," says Mottola. "Plus she's always gravitated toward that sound and culture."

Beyoncé Giselle Knowles-Carter was born and raised in Houston, a city where Latin—and especially Mexican—culture, food, and music is inescapable. Nearly half the population is Hispanic, with the population predicted to be majority Hispanic within four years. It's where Spanish is spoken on the streets, where Latin music has always been played on the radio, and where Tejana star Selena Quintanilla broke attendance records at the Astrodome.

"Beyoncé is grounded in her sense of which geographical heritage she should be paying homage to in her work," says Robinson. "We know from *Lemonade* and other albums that she is very much engaged in thinking about Louisiana as an inspirational site with an ancestral tribe from which she draws, but there's also her own coming of age in Houston, her own lived experience being a black girl in a city that has significant black and Latinx populations."

In a 2007 interview in *People en Español*, Beyoncé relayed that a close Mexican friend in Houston first introduced her to Selena's albums, which she then "listened to all the time." When she decided to record songs in Spanish, she consulted with a close Cuban friend to make sure her accent sounded authentic. "It may seem random to folks outside of the South that she sings in Spanish and nods to those roots, but she's from the Nuevo South, the Latinx South, and from that vantage point it makes complete and total sense," says Robinson.

If anyone else were to attempt what Robinson calls Beyoncé's synchronism of so many cultures, they might come off as an opportunist. Not Beyoncé. "When you sing in Spanish and try on our culture you run the risk of someone saying you're not doing it right and you aren't talking to us," says Leila Cobo, executive director of Latin Content at Billboard. "Beyoncé has never had that sort of backlash." Cobo cites Nat King Cole as providing historical precedence. "He recorded three albums that he executed with precision and authenticity, even recording in Cuba," says Cobo of the albums that were critically acclaimed bestsellers. "They are classics," confirms Mottola, who recounts a story about his wife, the Mexican artist Thalía. "When I met her mother, who only loves Mexican music, she proudly showed me her Nat King Cole Spanish albums. I couldn't believe it."

Like Cole, Beyoncé excels at her craft and she works hard at it, whether it's hours of diction training with Luis Fonsi's brother Jean Rodriguez for "*Mi Gente*," or making sure her best friend, a Cuban, approves of how she sings a Spanish love song. The respect shows. "She sees the music as really good music, as artistically interesting and having its own merit," says Cobo. "She doesn't measure Latin as a passing fad."

It's not a fad and I'm here for it. The Latin population is growing across the country and it is young (nearly 60 percent of U.S. Hispanics are millennial, according to the Pew Research Center), which means we are driving trends. In addition to Latin artists and Spanish-language songs charting higher and with more frequency than previous years, the streaming numbers show that Latin songs are in demand (two of Spotify's top five global playlists are Latin). Of course, it helps that Latin music increasingly slots into broader categories. "Latin music is more than the traditional definition now," says Mottola. "It's urban, pop, global." It's embodied at various intersections by artists like Amara La Negra, Snow tha Product, Bad Bunny, J. Balvin, Nicky Jam, Gente de Zona, and Kap G—and, yes, Beyoncé.

"It's the popular music of the time and our new culture," says Mottola. "It's the new America."

Style So Sacred

————◆————

EDWARD ENNINFUL

They wore jeans. Really tight jeans. The first time I saw Destiny's Child perform it was at Notting Hill Carnival in London. They were all dressed alike. I don't recall their tops, just their skintight jeans. A few months earlier I had first listened to their first album, which I played on repeat. They were all amazing, but I knew Beyoncé especially was going to be a star.

Beyond her voice, her talents, and her presence, Beyoncé is someone you know has had to work hard and strives for perfection. You can tell whatever she is now has come through hard work. I recognize and respect that part of who she is because nothing was handed to me on a plate. And while it's about perfecting your craft, it wasn't just the music that made her—it's about looking amazing and about the fashion choices made with each song. Her fashion choices have always been well thought out. You saw that early on with the bold and sexy looks in "Independent Women" and the coordinated army fatigues in "Survivor."

It was with her solo album, *Dangerously in Love*, that I knew she was going to be a fashion heavyweight. The styling of those videos—"Crazy in Love," "Bonnie and Clyde"—hypersexy but never vulgar, streetwear but at the same time designer, that perfect high-low mix, stunning hair and makeup, and her powerful attitude too, saw her transform at that moment into a bona fide fashion icon. I felt that was when she truly married her music with fashion.

Fashion always tells you about the times we're living in. Look at *Lemonade* with its powerful messages of independence and feminism told through the music and also the fashion, all of it relating to women. The feminine red, white, and black script-print silk Gucci dress she wears on top of the police car is one of my favorites. I was working as the creative director of *W* magazine at the time and had featured that same dress in an editorial that came out then. I remember thinking that she had picked the very dress that I had loved most from that collection. And of course the ruffled yellow silk Roberto Cavalli gown, in a richer hue than the baseball bat she carried, epitomized vibrancy and the feeling of being very alive (though scorned). But the scene on the porch in which she's wearing the black wide-brimmed hat low on her eyes, dressed in a fitted black gown, silver jewelry stacked high, with the men in black suits behind her, was perhaps the most powerful image, reflecting ideas of our independence and fight for freedom, a fight that is not yet over, expressed through the clothes.

When I think about her fashion choices on stage, in videos, and on the red carpet, Beyoncé is about celebrating womanhood. Even at this time in fashion that is partly defined by androgyny, she's never asexual and always deliberately feminine with her style choices, showcasing curves and female form. It's celebrating your female body, not being restricted by body shape, wearing what makes you feel great. She embraces herself as she is. Which is a reason why women love her so much. She's unapologetically herself and encourages other women to be the same way: *Wear what you want! Don't let society say you shouldn't wear this or that because of your shape! Just do it!* That's strength.

I've always found beauty in all shapes and sizes. It's the beautiful and proud Ghanaian women in my family who taught me what beauty is and that the world is such a better place because we're diverse. Beyoncé has always been a champion of diversity, of different kinds of beauty taking center stage. It's something I've championed too in the styling and fashion work I've done, from starting at *i-D* to the advertising campaigns and now at British *Vogue*. It's absolutely one of the reasons why I do admire and respect her so much. We have a responsibility. We have been lucky to have been given a platform and we don't take it lightly. I grew up with incredible women, all different body shapes, so to me that was the world, and I feel that Beyoncé was probably similar in that regard. Then we both sort of came up with our respective talents but have never forgotten where we come from or what our mothers and our grandmothers and our aunts look like. For me, and I imagine for Beyoncé, it's like second nature. We don't even have to think about inclusion and diversity, it's not planned, it just is.

While she flaunts her assets, she's never vulgar and this is an important point. I call it the "Beyoncé Sheen," which is when you put a certain level of chic on whatever super-sexy thing you are wearing, even super-short cutoffs. It's not learned, either, it's an innate trait that allows one to be extra sexy while being empowering and never a victim.

As an outsider to American culture, I also see her Texas roots showing through in her style. You see in her the whole idea of a cheerleader, which we don't have in England. Cheerleader fashion, majorette culture, that's all very American, and she channels that especially when she wears bodysuits. She is in fact the queen of the bodysuit. She brought that look to mainstream fashion so much so that it's reflected in her Ivy Park fashion line, a body-positive, youthful, and hip fashion line that also is a testament to her influence beyond music.

On the streets of London, Ivy Park has become a logo that's regularly visible. With its joggers and bodysuits and sports bras it's clearly an athleisure line, but it also exists beyond that categorization, reflecting how she's elevated and embraced street fashion.

At this point in her career and with the access to high fashion that she has, it would have been easy for her to explore any area of the industry, but choosing pieces with a lower price point proves her mission of inclusion and the unrivaled understanding of her audience. It's important to note also how every campaign since the launch in spring 2016 has featured young talent in its imagery, in particular women of color.

The imagery demonstrates her commitment to young women, but also to everyone else, to be who they are, to wear what they want to wear, stand for what they want to stand for. The gay community loves her for this, for her devotion to standing with us as well as for her glamour—the big hair, the beautiful makeup and body, the whole package. She's up there with Madonna, Streisand, Ross—all the greats. Being an ultimate gay icon will be part of her legacy.

When I travel the world, from Africa to South America to Europe, I see firsthand her global influence and how she is worshipped. Everyone the world over knows of her and is inspired by her aspirational qualities and the fact that she's made the world a better place by being in it. She will forever be a music icon, a fashion icon, a gay icon, an icon for young women, a diversity icon, and a philanthropist who gives back. All of this is Beyoncé. In fashion we talk about trends, but she's above trends. She can't be put in a box. Frankly, she can do whatever she wants.

The Beauty of Beyoncé

---◆---

FATIMA ROBINSON

When and Where I Enter

I was a kid who never stopped moving. I found movement in everything. I could sit in the lobby of a hotel and watch how everyone comes out of the elevator and walks through the door, the way the front-desk people do their job and make a dance sequence of it. Anything I see—it all feels like a choreographed movement, the way I move through life feels like a dance.

I graduated high school at sixteen, and in L.A. they had these clubs that had dance contests. It was the late 1980s, early 1990s—it was the beginning of hip hop, and dance was so important to the culture. I loved the music, and all the artists had dancers with them who made names for themselves too. I felt like the clubs were my church and I *had* to go. The dance floor was where I felt closest to God.

We were literally creating the new dance steps and the new trends. Now the kids do it with each other and they post it on YouTube and they create the next dance craze, but back then clubs were where crazes were born. Because I wasn't trained, spending hours on the dance floor, that's really where I kind of got my training. Dancers would come in from New York or Atlanta and we would all battle each other on the dance floor, but at the same time we're exchanging moves with each other, and just learning from each other. It was really such a great time.

Big Daddy Kane had his dancers: Scoop and Scrap. Queen Latifah had her two female dancers. Heavy D and the Boyz and Mary J. Blige always had dancers too. It's funny because hip hop dance back then, it wasn't considered a true art form. I would go to places like Alvin Ailey or a dance conservatory and they never really understood hip hop dance. But now hip hop dance is a preeminent form of dance—not just for young people but also for dance companies. It's amazing to know that it started with all these hip hop artists who brought on their dancers as part of the show.

Because we weren't part of the dance establishment, I never even used the term choreographer to describe myself. We were just putting together the show. You danced with someone, you made up the routine. Dance was just a natural part of any stage performance. I had to learn the counting process. For years, I taught to the lyrics or the beat of the music, because that's where it came from for me. Now, I'm more seasoned and trained and I know how to put everything to a count.

Remember the Time

I got my first big, *big* break choreographing the video for Michael Jackson's "Remember the Time." From there, it's been an amazing journey of working with artists, from those in the early part of their career to those wanting to achieve something that you know is a culmination of years of their creative evolution. I choreographed Aaliyah's "Rock the Boat" and Rihanna's first hit single, "Pon de Replay." Pharrell is a frequent collaborator and choreographing his 24-hour "Happy" video was a watershed moment for both of us.

Aaliyah and I were very close, personally and professionally. She came into the public eye around the same time as Destiny's Child, so they really were peers and respected each other. I think Aaliyah's work affected a lot of people. She was such an individual. She had her own lane, you know, and Destiny's Child had their lane, and then Beyoncé carved her lane out of that. Rihanna and I had that conversation when I first met her about how Aaliyah's career affected her and made her want to be an artist. Rihanna talked about how she would sing Aaliyah's songs. Even Drake has said, "I learned how to sing by singing to Aaliyah's music. That's why I sound the way I do in my singing voice." He told me, "I wasn't very comfortable with singing and I found it through listening to her music and singing along to her music."

My Introduction to Beyoncé

I've had the pleasure of working with Beyoncé since the days of Destiny's Child. It takes a lot to break into the entertainment industry, but even more tenacity to maintain your status, your presence, your fan base, your stamina, your good looks, and your sanity!!!!!

Beyoncé is the best performer since Michael Jackson. She is the new Michael Jackson. Michael was a template for a whole generation of dancers, but for me, he was also a template of a work ethic. When I choreographed "Remember the Time," I was 21 years old, and just being in the room with him, working with a perfectionist of his caliber, really set the tone for how I wanted to move forward in my career. Beyoncé has that same tenacity and the way in which she puts in the work is amazing. She makes everybody around her pull up. She works *so* hard. It's tough to find that type of work ethic. I've had artists in the room, names you know well, who can sing and they can dance, but they sit down and get on their phones between each take. That's not how Beyoncé rolls. A lot of people don't understand the level of intensity it takes to reach the points that she's reached. It takes turning off *everything* in the outside world and focusing on who *you* are as a performer, and executing the vision that comes from the deepest part of your soul.

It's this unknowable, inimitable combination of vision, imagination, and work ethic that makes her live stage performance come to life. People don't understand that even the simplest dance combination represents hours and hours and hours of doing it again and again and again and again. Then you step away from the mirror and come at it again for hours and hours the next day. It's like anything else, if you go to the gym every day and you put in that same amount of work every day, in a month you're going to be like "Wow, look at my body." You're going to put on your clothes like wow, this is fitting different. As a choreographer, it's wonderful to be in a room and see the artist master a trick, master something that they just couldn't get the day before.

A star has a special kind of energy. When I first started working with Rihanna, I went "Wow, this girl's a star." You see talent, but it's what you feel that really tells you.

There's a certain way that stars carry themselves that is quite unlike anything you've seen before, no matter how many times you've seen pure talent walk through the door. Artists like Rihanna, or Aaliyah, or Beyoncé don't feel like part of the crowd. They really stand out.

When I first worked with Beyoncé, I instantly felt her spirit. She had a fire in her that you rarely see in artists at such a young age. So often, you meet an artist and you see that there's talent, but you think, "Okay, now we've got to connect talent with business sense and work ethic and vision." When it all connects, time and again, you get the breakthrough   it's like "Ah, now they've made it." Whereas with a very select handful, and Beyoncé is prototypical in this way, you just see everything right there and right then.

When you go to her show you are not only entertained, you are transported into a world of fun, laughter, dance, and majesty. The lighting, incredible costumes, well-curated screen content, the elaborate set pieces, and the woman herself all make for an outstanding show. Her message of female empowerment stays with you long after and you feel like the queen you are.

Singing and Dancing Are Two Different Things

Let's be clear—not everyone who can sing, can dance. Some people are just better at one or the other. She's just one of those people who really understands dance and the language of it and the nuances of it. It's definitely rare that you get people who have both the ability to sing and dance at that level. That's why everyone is so entertained by that kind of artist—a Michael Jackson, a Prince, a Beyoncé—because *they are a rare bird.*

I was the choreographer on the feature film *Dreamgirls* where Beyoncé played Deena Jones—she was gorgeous in that film. She stunned the world with not only her singing and dancing in the movie, but with her courageous acting ability. In rehearsals she was a perfectionist. Staying hours to get every move right, every hand gesture, every head turn, every spin to the camera. Being a fellow Virgo, I know what that perfectionist bug feels like. She is a beast! I appreciated the hard work—hell, it made me work even harder. We spent every day together for months and I often got to hear about the love of her life—now husband—Jay-Z. I'd known Jay since I was eighteen when we went on tour all around the world with Big Daddy Kane. Jay played the hype man, and I did my thing—I danced.

I was so happy to hear that two greats had connected and

loved to see the glow in her eyes when she had a few days off to be with him. We need to applaud how she's made that marriage a testimony to the kind of realness that is the antithesis to most Hollywood relationships. Spilling her heart out to the world on her sixth solo album, *Lemonade,* by revealing the vulnerabilities in her relationship only made her/them stronger and better.

One of the gifts she has given us as an artist is to let us into her struggle and her emotional evolution. We get to dance and sing along as she digs into her truth and emerges unapologetic and loving herself—which, of course, gives us permission to do the same. When I went to the last concert it was interesting to see how many girl gangs there were. So many women collectively came together to go see Beyoncé and support her, but who also like to do those dances together and are like "Get me to the floor." To see women having fun with each other like that, without inhibitions, was so great. I think she's given so many women permission to be who they are and love who they are and live their life, perfect in their imperfections.

Coachella

Let's talk about Coachella for a minute. I'm the daughter of a woman who went to Tennessee State. My mother was a majorette and my father played in the band. Beyoncé's performance—her loving tribute to historically Black colleges and universities—

touched my heart. Coachella wasn't ready for the level of realness her performance brought—from the bleacher stage design to the fireworks hitting during the crescendo of the horn section, to the nonstop dance that made you have to move and sing along, to the way in which the songs were remixed to fit the festival crowd. It was a masterful execution of a stage show with hundreds of moving pieces. As Questlove tweeted: *"How. in. The. Fuh. Did. She. Pull. That. Shiii. OFF!!!!??? It's like 170 musicians onstage. I mean the stage plotting. The patch chords. How many monitor boards were used??! Bandleading that shit woulda gave me anxiety. Hats off man. Jesus H Christ."*

Albert Einstein once said "dancers are the athletes of God." As dancers, we push our bodies to do different and new things, and there is *creation* at every level when you are working with the greats. Sometimes you have days when it goes smoothly and the creative moves come to you and it's all good, and some days you're stuck and you're trying to figure out how to make it better, or something just isn't feeling right. Sometimes you have to leave it and come back to it with a fresh eye. I know Beyoncé does that a lot, she does skeleton crews of work where you only hire a few dancers to help you ideate the piece. For a job like Coachella, say if there were over 100 dancers onstage, she may do a skeleton crew with just 15 of them. Then you do a skeleton layout of where you want the piece to go, which then helps you kind of orchestrate the music and orchestrate the stage plan. From there, you keep building and building and building. There are many layers to orchestration: figuring out what works and what doesn't work; sometimes you come back the next day and say, "That formation doesn't work. These moves look better in this formation. Or if we move this piece of the choreography over there, we could steal this piece." It's like emptying a clock, shaking all the pieces out onto the desk, then putting it back together until it runs. Choreography at that level is tweezer work.

It's easier to make a name for yourself than it is to sustain it. To sustain it, you have to constantly grow and reinvent yourself. Decades from now, Americans will be talking about Beyoncé at Coachella, the way we remember Diana Ross performing in Central Park in the rain, Michael Jackson popping up from the scoreboards at the Super Bowl, or Josephine Baker at the Folies Bergère in Paris, dancing her heart out in that infamous banana dress.

Not only is Beyoncé a megastar, but she's a mother, sister, wife, friend, and role model to countless fans who look up to her, ask advice, or just use her as the inspiration they need to conquer whatever is going on in their lives. As a mother, she does the delicate dance of not exposing her kids to too much too fast. As a sister, she is there to always support Solange, who was too young to be in Destiny's Child but had goals of being an entertainer in her own right. As a young girl with two younger sisters I often made up dance routines to perform for our mom when she had guests. Some of the routines that you see in *Dreamgirls* I cultivated in those early years with my sisters. The sisterly bond is a special one and watching Bey and Solange perform together always reminds me of those tender times of bonding with my sisters. As we have gotten older the wonderful relationship has allowed us to grow and go our separate ways but always support each other too. When I watch videos of Beyoncé as a child, it reminds me of myself, and I attribute both our successes to the amazing matriarchs of our families: Ms. Tina Knowles and my mother, Khadijah Lewis. Their leadership and guidance has given us the strength to push through and taught us life lessons to help achieve our goals that we then pass on to our children.

Unpacking Her Ancestry

Black Excellence is what Beyoncé has always stood for. When she tells you to move your butt or get in formation you do it!! She always stays true to who she is; she never ignores the culture but consistently brings it to the forefront, educating people about who we are and what we do. As a culture creator, she is constantly evolving, pushing the boundaries and exploring unchartered territory. That's what great artists do and whether I'm working with Pharrell Williams or Kendrick Lamar, I help bring their vision to life, always pushing them to be better. The creative process is an exciting one. Critiquing yourself until you get it right, recognizing when something doesn't sit in what we like to call "that pocket." Questioning how performances will impact people emotionally yet still be entertaining. Getting inside the head of an artist, inside the lyrics and meaning of a song, while always asking the question, "What do we want to convey to the audience?"

One of the things you've seen in Beyoncé's work is the unpacking and elevating of her ancestry. Once I started taking African dance classes, it changed everything. The teacher would tell us the roots of these dances, and they were so similar to what we did in hip hop. I kept thinking, "This is so crazy. We're actually just doing something that comes from our ancestry, not even knowing."

Why Beyoncé's Work Feels Like Home

In the beginning of our careers, dancers travel the world, we never leave our hotel, we eat at McDonald's all over the world, it's pretty awful. It's not even just the dancers, it's any young artist, any new artist. You can tell there was a shift when Beyoncé started to really open her eyes to what's around her, and be exposed to art and other cultures and dance on an international level. You started to see a new ownership in her artistry as she began to incorporate a kind of dance that stayed true to her, that felt right to her, even though it drew on entirely new inspiration. It's like, Oh, wow, this is interesting. I'm all the way over here, but for some reason this move feels like home. I need to introduce this into my music, into my world, into my art. With Beyoncé, it's just nonstop evolution and growth. A lot of times what I do in an artist's life and career is I give them permission to do what they are already yearning to do. They just may be a little scared and timid about it, or not sure if it's the right way to go. And I help push that forward. When an artist like Beyoncé trusts her instincts and has the courage to follow her curiosity, that's when the magic comes in. We respond to Beyoncé the way we do because we're getting to be a part of her growth, which is rare—and wonderful.

Because Beyoncé.

———◆———

EBRO DARDEN

Ask anything about her, it doesn't matter: her life, her music, her career. At the end of the day, the answer is always: "Because Beyoncé."

I was 23 the first time I heard of her. That was 20 years ago, when I was the program director at one of the biggest radio stations in Sacramento, California. I got the Destiny's Child, "No, No, No," single from Sony, and while the record was cool and people liked it, it was the remix with Wyclef Jean that truly blew up. Then the video came out and that was it: Beyoncé was visibly and vocally a standout.

The music they were doing was young, and they looked like what was happening right then in the clubs and in the street. But what I liked and noticed the most was that Beyoncé wasn't trying to be soft like some of the other acts in the late nineties.

She was pioneering something new with a record that was hip hop but also mainstream. And of course, it had a lot of different elements, which has always been one of the great things about her music. But above all, that record was a strong record and Beyoncé sounded strong. The album left you wanting more of that music and especially more of her.

Then in 1999, she gave us more, much more. That's when the songs started getting stronger, talking all that shit to men with *The Writing's on the Wall* album, and "Bills, Bills, Bills," "Bug A Boo," "Jumpin', Jumpin'," and "Say My Name." The music sounded fresh and amplified the message of women not taking shit, and we were singing along. I remember listening to "Say My Name," and being compelled emotionally by the lyrics. It was a girl's conversation, sure, but as a man you felt like, "Yo, what do you mean pay my bills? Can you pay my . . . like, who are you talking to?"

That's when it became abundantly clear too that Beyoncé would embrace the bold while lyrically tapping into whatever was happening culturally and was real. Cute and timid is not her thing.

And, frankly, how can Beyoncé, as a grown woman, ever be cute or timid? Vocally she can't help but sound aggressive yet simultaneously sexy. That's a rare talent. Think about her delivery. When you listen to Beyoncé's recordings it sounds like she's performing in front of you. She *is* the record. That's something only the greats like Tina Turner have the ability to do. In fact, and like many people, I see a lot of Tina Turner in Beyoncé—the way she has her legs out, her energy onstage. There are other influences too, like the pop success of a Whitney, the hip hop and R&B vibes of an Aaliyah. You see Janet Jackson in Beyoncé too, with the dancers and the big productions. She's pulling from some of the great soul artists from Chaka Khan to Aretha.

There's a way in songs like "Apesh*t" when she says, "suck my dick" or as "King Bey" that she is incorporating a masculine demeanor, but it's common in around-the-way girls and in the street. It's meant to be disrespectful. It's meant to be condescending. It's meant to be all of that. It's fun. It's just talking shit. I think for women, when she's Beyoncé, the badass, it reminds them that she's still herself despite being a mom with three kids. Despite being one of the most famous women on planet Earth she can still be just like them and not give a sh*t. There's the element of yes, *I got all this money and I don't have to fuck with people who don't understand our shit.*

Beats 1 has been an incredible education in what and how music is interpreted around the world. I started working there the day it turned on in June 2015. I've spent my whole career in radio but I never imagined that I would anchor a radio show that would be heard in over 100 countries, simultaneous streaming—so many people in every time zone in the world, listening to the same songs at the same time.

I see my job as finding and delivering entertaining content to people. I see myself as a conduit, kind of like a middleman if you will. The job of a DJ is to present music in a way that is consumable and digestible and give it some context.

What I've learned the most in this role is the power of hip hop internationally.

I can't help but notice the inclusive fan base Beyoncé has

built here and internationally. Beyoncé. Even her name has some of the Creole heritage, which obviously has French ties through slavery and Africa and all of that. And then you see her affection for Paris, which is absolutely mutual. She's like that city, she's a cultural epicenter.

People think that the first big move of African Americans to Paris began with Josephine Baker and then later the Harlem Renaissance, but it goes back even further—to the Louisiana Purchase of 1803. And Louisiana takes you right back to Beyoncé and her Creole roots.

For so many African American artists, Paris has been a refuge. Paris is amazing but it's definitely classist. It's like any other place where there are rich and poor and the completely disenfranchised.

Beyoncé enters a room and she never leaves her Blackness behind, the way she absolutely could as a celebrity. She did it with "Apesh*t" being shot at the Louvre. In the Louvre Black people are almost exclusively depicted as slaves. The gold in the streets of Paris is stolen from Africa. The obelisks are African and the pyramid imagery is African. Paris has stolen from Africa. The people that built it are stolen from Africa. Then the art in the Louvre only depicts Black people as possessions.

I believe Beyoncé shot that video in the Louvre because she and Jay are a living art installation of Blackness and Africanness. They turned that statement into a music video that will live on forever.

I don't belong to a lot of the social groups that she talks to, but throughout her discography she's made sure to incorporate certain language, different dances, and different video elements that signal to anyone who watches or listens that she's reaching out to them, acknowledging them. That's another one of her superpowers.

Still Beyoncé isn't for everybody, apparently. Case in point: She hasn't won a Grammy for Album of the Year. How many times do we have to be reminded about the imbalance in cultural understanding in America? She's built this huge popularity across multitudes of tribes and created critically amazing records, but she hasn't won a Grammy for Album of the Year. Something like 14,000 Grammy voters vote on this category and, for better or worse, it's not just people who pay attention to popular music. They didn't get it right, I know that. Even Adele, who famously won against her in 2017, knows it and said as much to the world. But with the Grammys, the people who have voting power just aren't paying attention to mainstream media and mainstream consumption of music; they are literally voting based just on what they know.

Lemonade includes multiple genres of music. The way it was released was different. It was very groundbreaking in a lot of ways and just as we see in politics, the new is a struggle. That said, I do believe that if the album had been produced by someone white, those new ideas would be embraced more. It's a double whammy that you have a Black woman who reinforces the idea that she doesn't care what anybody thinks and releases an album the way she wants to on her husband's streaming service.

And now look at what they did to Jay-Z at the Grammys in 2018, when he released his album on Tidal. You've got to ask: do these voters have a problem with Jay and Bey controlling their own destiny and the release of their music the way they do?

Fortunately, one of Beyoncé's other great superpowers is her ability to fight. She gets knocked down by life and gets up again and wins. So no doubt the shelf without an Album of the Year Grammy gives her a reason to keep working and gives us a reason to keep in formation with her. And she will and we—her fans and especially those who have grown up alongside her—will be part of that journey just as we always have been.

Beyoncé has shared her journey with us. In this day and age of transparency, her fans have grown up with her. That's a lot of life to live in front of people, and we are grateful for the superpower of bravery and humility that allowed her to let us bear witness.

Because Beyoncé has spent decades developing a deep relationship with her fans, she's earned a level of trust and respect from us. We live in a country driven by polarization. Though Beyoncé may not be standing on a soapbox, she's not afraid to speak out through her music and actions. She's shown incredible solidarity with President Barack Obama and Michelle Obama. She's shown solidarity with people who are speaking out against police brutality. She's shown solidarity with Colin Kaepernick. She's shown solidarity with the Black Nationalist movement through the repeated use of Black Panther imagery.

And Black people know what kind of risk that is. On the fiftieth anniversary of the Black Panthers—a group that at one time was seen by the FBI as a threat to the American way of life—Beyoncé walked out at the biggest televised event ever and put her fist in the air and wore an afro to pay homage. And to the detractors that bubbled up and tried to stand in opposition to her: Black people know exactly what people were trying to do to discredit her. Detractors were trying to frame and create a narrative that somehow she's problematic or disrespectful to American society. They criticized her because she paid homage to people who came from a similar community as she came from and she honored a community who had to fight and pave a path for Black people to have respect from law enforcement and the government. For one of the biggest stars on the planet Earth to go out and put her fist in the air, that, in our eyes, is literally risking everything. That she put herself on the line for all of us is another of her superpowers.

Think about how many times we've seen a Black celebrity speak up for people who were being oppressed, specifically Black people, and be either criticized or ostracized or both. That's happening right now to Colin Kaepernick—he can't get a job. But because Beyoncé is self-made and works for herself, she is immune for the most part from being pulled down. That untouchability is something very few Black people in America know. Most of us have always held jobs where we work for someone else. If we step out of line or do anything that's seen as controversial, we're expendable. But you can't get rid of Beyoncé. There's nothing anyone can do to prevent Beyoncé from talking to her fans and putting out music. She releases music videos the way she wants to. She releases her music the way she wants to.

Worldwide, Beyoncé means beautiful, Black, strong woman. She means powerful. She means self-made, successful. I am a proud member of the Beyhive. I respect her work ethic and loyalty and the way she stands her ground.

I respect her for my daughter, who turned four this year. She will always have not only the discography of Beyoncé but all of the visual material and the live performances of someone who transcended all the obstacles and became an icon and whose complexion and hair texture are similar to hers. That's a gift, when you can see yourself in someone else.

However you want to look at this superstar, what you'll always come back to is simple: "Because Beyoncé."

King Bey

TREVA B. LINDSEY

Get off my dick." I literally laughed out loud when I first heard this line in "Apesh*t." The cockiness (all puns intended) of the demand amid talking about her expensive fabrics and habits and having the ability to make a person famous after hanging out with her for just one night amused me in both its honesty and its well-earned arrogance. Not a single lie detected in her declarations about her wealth and fame. Absent from this song, and more specifically her verses and the chorus, is any semblance of humility or modesty. She fully embraces a self-assuredness so few Black women can publicly embody without paying a very hefty price. I was in awe of this unflinching and unapologetic confidence. She modeled what Pulitzer Prize–and Grammy Award–winning artist Kendrick Lamar rapped: "I can't fake humble cause your ass is insecure." Beyoncé came to slay.

"Apesh*t" was by no means the first time Beyoncé sang or rap-sung about her prowess or commanded people to respect her grind and accomplishments. The lead single off of her joint album with her husband and frequent collaborator, Jay-Z, simply exemplifies a performance bravado she began cultivating in the 1990s and commenced showing off in the 2010s: King Bey. This shit-talking, boastful, and brash persona inhabited by Beyoncé is one of the most intriguing and perhaps unexpected developments in her storied 20-plus year career. She had been bootylicious, a diva, and even a Queen—but the creation and evolution of King Bey signaled a turn toward a new chapter in her inimitable career. *Everything Is Love* offers a body of work in which Beyoncé claims a distinct place within hip hop via King Bey as a fully realized performance persona.

Throughout Beyoncé's career, hip hop, and particularly Southern hip hop, played and continues to play an integral role in her visual, sonic, style, and dance aesthetics. Whether collaborating with Wyclef Jean on the remix to Destiny's Child's first single or popping up in a Willie D video, Beyoncé's connection to hip hop is undeniable. While I'm hesitant to call her a hip hop artist, her albums, music videos, and concerts would be unrecognizable without what she pulls from hip hop culture. Her pop star appeal never quieted her desire to work with rappers or to connect with an audience uninterested in radio-friendly, urban pop songs.

There's not a point in her career in which Beyoncé has not been associated with hip hop music culture. In 1993, when her first girl group, Girls Tyme, secured a spot on the "greatest talent competition show ever," *Star Search*, host Ed McMahon introduced the six young Black girls as a "hip hop, rappin' group." Although there was and in some cases still is a tendency to identify young Black artists as rappers regardless of what genre they actually perform, the energetic performance was influenced by the choreography, fashion, and rhythmic flow of nineties hip hop. A twelve-year-old Knowles knew how to ride the beat. The group lost. Not long after, the lineupchanged and the group reconfigured into the original lineup of Destiny's Child. Twenty years later, the footage and sound byte of Girls Tyme losing on *Star Search* played a pivotal role on *Beyoncé*, the visual album as the intro and outro for her empowering and shit-talking anthem, "***Flawless."

The debut of Destiny's Child is inextricably linked to hip hop as well. It's not just that the first video off of their debut album featured rapper-producer Wyclef Jean, it's that they used the more hip hop–influenced remix of "No, No, No," to introduce themselves to a national audience. A staple in hip hop, particularly in the 1990s, the remix in many cases surpasses the original in popularity. "No, No, No" was no exception. Beyoncé took the reins and rode what Wyclef called in the music video a "phat beat for the clubs." The remix of the soulful track exhibited what became a signature element of both Destiny's Child's and Beyoncé's vocal performances, an almost rap-sing quality to her delivery. Her rapid singing, distinct phrasing, and effortless shifts between breathy, soulful notes and percussive and sharp vocal execution make her one of the most distinct voices in modern pop music. Beyoncé is a singer who draws on soul, R&B, and pop traditions—but her unwavering relationship to hip hop always contributes to her unique sound as well.

Destiny's Child never shied away from the influence of hip hop in their production or their style, therefore it was unsurprising that when Beyoncé temporarily broke off from the group, hip hop played an integral role in her solo efforts. Prior to dropping her first album in 2003, she recorded the lead single, "Work It Out," for the soundtrack for her film *Austin Powers in Goldmember.* Months later, the lead single from the soundtrack of another one of her films, *Fighting Temptations,* dropped, featuring female rappers Missy Elliott, MC Lyte, and Free. Beyoncé ended the year with a feature on her then-rumored boyfriend's (Jay-Z) track "'03 Bonnie & Clyde." The ride-or-die track reached number four on the Billboard Hot 100 and sparked even more interest in a post–Destiny's Child Beyoncé album.

On June 24, 2003, Beyoncé doubled down on her affinity for hip hop by releasing the first track off her debut solo album, *Dangerously in Love,* "Crazy in Love," featuring Jay-Z. The playful pop song with a side of hip hop launched Beyoncé into the pop stratosphere, where she remains. One of the more R&B-influenced and entrenched entries in her six-album discography, *Dangerously in Love* includes two collaborations with Jay-Z as well as features from rap artists Missy Elliott and Big Boi. Elliott, alongside hip hop and R&B producers Rich Harrison and Scott Storch, also played significant roles in shaping the sound of Beyoncé's debut album. *Dangerously in Love* went on to become a critically acclaimed and commercially successful album, garnering Knowles five Grammys, Billboard Music awards, and numerous nominations. She bet on soul and hip hop as vehicles for making her pop music distinct from her peers. She won.

With each album, tour, and televised performance, Beyoncé's stardom and fandom grew, as did her unabashed love and appreciation for hip hop collaborations. When reuniting with Destiny's Child in 2004, one of their most memorable and commercially successful singles off their last album, *Destiny Fulfilled*, was "Soldier." In the song and music video, which features rap artists such as T.I., Lil' Wayne, and Ice Cube, she brags about the kind of guys they like, and the song contains Beyoncé's not-so-subtle, flirtatious lyrics about her lover, Jay-Z. Hip hop bravado became increasingly audible and visible in her music, videos, and concerts as Beyoncé experimented with new sounds, choreography, and vocal techniques.

After her first couple of solo projects, Beyoncé gradually introduced the world to her alter ego, Sasha Fierce. As Sasha, Beyoncé became a force—a playfully shit-talking diva with a big ego and Black girl sass. As Beyoncé's popularity grew, so did the monikers for her. Each moniker for Beyoncé—Queen Bey, Yoncé, or Baddie Bey—carried with it a specific meaning. Many of the monikers toyed with hip hop posturing and played with the kind of overt confidence often associated with rap artists. King Bey, the latest addition to the list, encapsulates both Bey's history with hip hop and her more recent turn toward rapping and rap bravado as a space of expression, not just of collaboration.

In 2013 her sound and styling took a deep dive into the creation of King Bey. The song was "Bow Down/I Been On."

Instantly, the track enticed and repulsed. While many applauded her experimentation with rap-singing, the chopped and screwed second verse, and comparatively more explicit lyrics, the backlash to her percussive insistence that "bitches bow down" was equally swift. After proclaiming that girls run the world, more than a few people balked at the idea that Beyoncé could turn around and make a song in which she brags about telling her crew to "smack that trick." I enjoyed Beyoncé before this single, but I became a fan once it dropped. This song, the accompanying visuals, and the starkly different responses to it signaled a creative risk and a seductive audacity that endeared Beyoncé to me as an artist. She and her team dared to play a new game and gamble with the expectations of her devoted and still-growing fan base.

While it was Queen Bey who demanded that bitches bow down, it was King Bey, with this studio-created, masculine voice, that reminisced about her girlhood in Houston and mused about stunting in her "gold everything." Her memories of having dookie braids alongside her confessing to sneaking to listen to UGK are enlivened through her usage of chopped and screwed, a sound originated in Houston in the late 1980s and early 1990s by the late DJ Screw. It's a performance rooted in her hometown and her complex relationship to the working-class Black culture of her city as a middle-class African American child and teenager. As Regina Bradley notes in "I Been On (Ratchet)," what Beyoncé offers on this track is a persona. Although initially identified as Baddie Bey, this persona is an introduction and formative precursor to King Bey.

For Beyoncé's groundbreaking self-titled visual album,

Knowles-Carter reinvented "Bow Down/I Been On" into "Flawless," a women's empowerment bop. Queen Bey returned with
a track with a sample of acclaimed author Chimamanda Ngozi
Adichie's TED Talk on feminism and a couple perfect catch-
phrases for the 2010s. The cultural resonance of "I woke up like
this" can't be overstated. Beyoncé took a song criticized by many
for its anti-feminist tone and content and transformed it into a
signature anthem. With "Flawless," Queen Bey became a pivotal figure in pop culture feminism. Although the song and
visual album were closely linked to the Queen Bey persona, it
was the King Bey ethos—one deeply wedded to audacity and
self-assurance—that powered Beyoncé's response to her critics
via the remaking of "Bow Down/I Been On." She was not back-
ing or bowing down on her declarations of being pop culture
royalty.

King Bey resurfaced on her latest solo album, the visually
arresting and musically diverse *Lemonade*. In one of the most
playful yet honest songs about infidelity and being fed up with
her partner, she rap-sings "suck on my balls, pause." This moment is so hip hop. Countless hip hop artists use "suck my
dick" and other vernacular terms for fellatio as a means of de-
meaning, deriding, or dismissing the subject of their ire. The
presence of the reference to balls or later her "dick" isn't what
makes her King Bey. King Bey emerges when she dabbles in
hip hop's unique vernacular. "Suck on my balls" or "get off my
dick" could undeniably be read as Beyoncé reproducing some
of the harmful, misogynist, homophobic, and sexist wordplay
extant in hip hop. While that is a valid critique, it is also possible to read this as Beyoncé claiming a throne within hip

hop—a music genre dominated by men. She enters the space as both King and Queen Bey, something not even her husband—one of the greatest rappers of all time—can do.

Everything Is Love is the most explicitly hip hop project in Beyoncé's discography. It conjoins Queen and King Bey. Some of the most memorable moments are those in which her hip hop bravado predominates. Whether singing "I can do anything" or "I'm Malcolm X," Beyoncé has entered a new chapter in her still-unfolding legendary career. More than any of her personas or former alter egos, King Bey reflects Beyoncé's love for hip hop. From the posturing to lyrical delivery, hip hop is interwoven into nearly every aspect of this chapter of her career. In her most recent tour, On the Run II, Beyoncé seamlessly moves among her various personas, but it is King Bey who closes the show. She shuts it down by effortlessly riding the beat on "Apesh*t." Beyoncé exits the stage knowing that she simultaneously reigns over both a Queendom and a Kingdom. There's no pop culture precedent for an artist being identified as both King and Queen. She breaks the rules, which only adds to her hip hop bravado. Beyoncé's trajectory to icon is one rooted in self-transformation as a performer. Her refusal to remain complacent or fixed as an entertainer, an artist, and a collaborator significantly contributes to her unprecedented success. At this point, Beyoncé primarily competes with herself—so why not be both King and Queen?

Meridional: Beyoncé's Southern Roots and References

ROBIN M. BOYLORN

Music is medicinal for my melancholy moods, but Beyoncé was not on my playlist or my radar when she launched her solo career, the year I turned 25. By then I had already left the rural landscapes of Chatham County, North Carolina, for the peninsula of Florida. Leaving had felt like an escape and a rescue because my biggest fear was shrinking myself enough to be swallowed by the hollowness of my hometown. Florida was farther south, but it didn't feel meridional. Pine trees were traded for palm trees, and the thick, humid heat of Florida summers was relieved by brief daily rain showers that would bathe me in public, almost always catching me by surprise, always almost cooling me off.

The next place I lived took me from the old South to the deep South. Alabama felt achingly familiar when I drove up from Tampa, through Tallahassee, Dothan, Montgomery, and into Tuscaloosa. Alabama was to be a reprieve, a place for me to reinvent myself, settle into my independence, learn how to make a living on my own, and curate a life bigger than what had previously felt possible. By then Beyoncé had put out two more albums and many more anthems. By then Beyoncé was a household name, exoticized instead of ghettoized because of her physical beauty and crossover appeal.

Her carefully crafted public persona was never without a reference to her Houston beginnings. Hardly home but always repping, Beyoncé, like me, always stayed close to home, metaphorically if not literally. Conspicuous sonic signifiers of the south seeped out in the Southern drawl of her speaking voice, the Houstonian accent in her spoken words on tracks, her collaboration with down South hip hop heads like Andre 3000, Bun B, and Slim Thug, and the visual and iconic imagery of southscapes she offered in music videos. Shout-outs and subtle Southern innuendoes had always been present in her work, but in her fifth and eponymous album, she seemingly went from "repping" where she was from to representing where she was from.

Aisha Durham, a Black feminist cultural critic, characterizes Beyoncé as the Southern belle of hip hop culture whose southernness is epitomized in her public performances of Southern femininity and self-perception. While Beyoncé's cultural currency had always transcended the South, in 2013, after the internet release of "Bow Down/I Been On," she doubled down on her Southern sound with an embrace of dirty South/trap music as a way of acknowledging and owning her full country self—complications, contradictions, and all. In that song, later released as the first part of "Flawless" on her self-titled album, Beyoncé reintroduced herself as someone who was not only from the South, but who identified with the South—and its affiliated and working-class aesthetics. The South, whether urban or rural, is often associated with poverty-stricken communities, rurality, retrograde thinking, and conservative religiosity. There are also assumptions that most Southerners are white. Beyoncé resists problematic presumptions by presenting the South as a main character in her work instead of letting it be blurred in the background. Through the imagery of Black bodies in various hues and contexts, her visual compilations mix opulence and deficiency like sugar syrup in sweet tea. Instead of compartmentalizing characterizations of Blackness in the South, she mashes them together—young and old, city and country, holy and secular, cis and trans, light skinned and dark, heterosexual and queer, public and private, but all Black—inviting her global audience to a new way of seeing and understanding American Southern culture.

Cultural understandings of the dirty South are both regional and class-based, so while Beyoncé grew up in a traditional, cishet home in a middle-class neighborhood she is still able to access and signify ratchetness (behavior linked to the ghettoization of Black womanhood) and respectability—simultaneously, and without the threat or impression of co-optation or appropriation. She embodies ratchet respectability, a hybrid of ratchetness and respectability politics that attempts to disprove some stereotypes (about Black women) while embracing others. With a backdrop of the Black South, Beyoncé teased her sixth studio album, *Lemonade*, with the unexpected release of "Formation," a song and video that embraced stereotypic conceptions of the South by centering them.

The song and video feature the Louisiana-laced voices of Messy Mya and Big Freedia. Their words and recognizable accents are inflected with inadvertent authenticity and lend credence to the song's intention to be(come) a Southern anthem. The refrain, which reminds us where her parents are from and where she was raised, offers additional evidence that Beyoncé's goal is to center and celebrate Southern Black culture and her Southern Black lineage. By identifying herself as a "Texas Bama," she charts a trifecta trajectory of the South: Texas, Alabama, and Louisiana. She also manages to situate preferences for soul food, baby hair, Negro noses, and hot sauce not only as Black, but Southern Black. Donning luxuriously long microbraids while leaning out of the window of an El Camino, Beyoncé is juxtaposed against Black women with colored weaves in a beauty supply store, scenes from a Black church and Black spirituality, representations of Southern goth, an all-Black marching band, a Black man wearing a cowboy hat on a horse, and Black women dressed in white holding hand fans as we shift from weatherworn homes drowned by floodwaters to a group of Black women twerking in the parlor of an ancient mansion. Each tableau is steeped in Southern jargon and repeated in the visual accompaniment to *Lemonade*, which features Beyoncé alongside an assemblage of Black women in the "country." The visuals and voice-overs ("earned all this money, but they'll never take the country out me") echo that no matter how successful she is, she will always be a country girl.

With the inclusion of a traditional country song on *Lemonade*, Beyoncé insisted that the ownership of country music is not limited to white people in Nashville, or Black men in the dirty South. "Daddy Lessons," a track about the advice a wayward father gives to his daughter about "men like him," includes all the trappings of a country song, including straightforward storytelling and references to evangelical Christianity, guns, and relationships. Despite the success of the song, including an invitation for Beyoncé to perform at the Country Music Awards in 2016, it was rejected by the Recording Academy's country music committee and was therefore ineligible for a Grammy award nomination in the country music categories—a seeming rejection of her efforts at portraying herself or her brand as country. Her foray into the country music realm was met with skepticism from some (who claimed it wasn't "country enough"), and support from others (who say it was "classic country"). Despite the disputes, the song, which was later covered by the country group Dixie Chicks, proves Beyoncé's artistry crosses boundaries and genres—and that the Southern roots and references of Bey's music catalogue are expansive enough to include handclaps and two-steps.

Lemonade was a serenade to Black women and an ode to the South. By privileging and finding the beauty in spaces and bodies often disappeared or made ugly in mainstream media, Beyoncé created a visually stunning portrait of the South with a gaze that focused on how we see ourselves rather than how we are perceived by others. This Southern subjectivity offered visibility and recognition by telling Black women's stories that centered rather than excluded them. As a project, *Lemonade* was unapologetically Black-woman centered and focused, a personalized open letter to our resilience, and an invitation for self-love and acceptance—it channeled the rural roots of Blackness and resonance of Black women's intergenerational, diasporic experiences.

Beyoncé poured metaphorical *Lemonade* in a see-through pitcher, like a see through picture, and made me feel vulnerable, but visible—a visibility that reverberated in the Black community, but especially for those of us located in the South, those of us who grew up in the South, those of us who recognized our mothers, grandmothers, and sisters in the story line.

By privileging things that are otherwise aesthetically displeasing, she used the lens of the camera to capture the essence of the Black experience.

Every still image was resonant. While experimenting with dual identities, Beyoncé navigated multiple spaces—from vast open fields, dilapidated ghettos, plantation homes, and parking lots she explored geographical space and landscapes, locating the South as more than urban or concrete, but also rural and red mud. Her reclamation of the South in *Lemonade* was consistent with the shifts of her work in recent years toward Blackness, feminism, and social justice activism—all of which appear in the visual album. She reiterates and reconciles her roots by marking her Southern identity in the tradition of blues women, Black feminists, and foremothers, all with legacies long buried in Southern ground.

The residue and legacies of the South will undoubtedly

continue to be central to Beyoncé's work, but *Lemonade* was something special, something magical. It awakened my own commitment to intentionally ground my work in my Southern identity. It reminded me of how powerful it is to know who we are, where we come from, and to whom we belong. Beyoncé's embrace of Black womanhood seeped in Southernness was a reminder that she sees us, and that she is one of us.

B & V: A Love Letter

---·---

CAROLINE CLARKE

It was April 2004—in a land before *Lemonade*, Blue, Rumi, or Sir. In fact, the future Mrs. Carter was still Beyoncé Knowles back then and, while Bey was big, her hive wasn't fully formed yet, and neither was she.

She was 22, crazy in love with her then-boyfriend Jay-Z, and had already been performing her heart out for more than half her life. She was the age she would have been graduating from college, had she chosen a more conventional path. But there was little conventional about Beyoncé Giselle Knowles—not her name, not her beauty (or much-celebrated booty), and not her outsized talent.

Exacting when it came to work, excellence was her default. Yet, humble and ladylike in interviews, it was easy to mistake her ferocious ambition for mere eagerness to please. In fact, back then it was easy to underestimate her altogether.

Her quirks—the deep-throated laugh that was a little goofy and her inability to wrangle that Houston accent—kept her real, even vulnerable, and made you want to give her a hug. But her hungry eyes, and the extreme care with which she did *everything*, gave her away.

At the tail end of a two-year hiatus from Destiny's Child, Beyoncé was commanding near-sellout crowds as she tested the solo waters in the wake of her debut album, *Dangerously in Love*. Released in 2003, it opened at No. 1 on the Billboard 200 albums chart, selling at bow-down speed: 300,000 copies in its first week.

Despite its global success and her growing comfort level slaying onstage without her sidekicks Kelly Rowland and Michelle Williams, Beyoncé seemed torn about cutting the cord with the group, which had become iconic in its own right. Having grown up with these girls, whom she calls sisters to this day, when asked about leaving them, the normally hyper-composed ingénue would sometimes struggle not to cry.

Managed by her father, Mathew, styled by her mother, Tina, and raised with Rowland and her baby sister, Solange, Beyoncé understood that Destiny's Child, with its stack of Grammys and fervent female following, was a force, and a pretty sure ticket to ride. The fact that it was also a family business where the family was close and business was booming made it especially hard to say bye. But mastering hard stuff—especially the stuff of which stars are made—was Beyoncé's chosen way of life.

Her Houston-based girl group rebounded mightily from its

1993 loss on TV's *Star Search,* where a prepubescent Beyoncé took the lead on vocals but didn't exactly shine. When I first saw the clip at the top of her 2013 *Flawless* video, I tipped my inner hat in respect. The irony was clever, but her willingness to out her own early failure was part of what made swelling legions of fans place her on a pedestal—a throne, in fact—in a stratosphere all her own.

I was a novice magazine editor in 1993, working alongside my husband and in-laws at their company, Black Enterprise. Like young Bey, I had learned a thing or two about mixing business and family. But, newly pregnant with my first child, I had no idea—*none*—how completely my life was about to change.

Born with a penetrating gaze and a headful of jet hair, my baby girl looked so much like me that my doting parents kept accidentally calling her by my name. From the start, though, Veronica Nicole Graves was entirely her own unduplicatable self. Even before she could walk or talk, she had an all-seeing, all-knowing quality that seriously gave me pause.

"An old soul," the elders would say, but it was more than that. Looking into her eyes as I held her close, I prayed that I would know enough, and *be* enough, to guide her through. I had never before felt so powerful, or so small.

Soon enough, we found our groove and, from the beginning, it had its own sweet soundtrack crooned straight from the heart by me: lullabies and kiddie tunes like "The Wheels on the Bus" and "You Are My Sunshine"; the Charlie Chaplin–penned heartbreaker "Smile" (covered best in my shameless opinion by my grandfather, Nat King Cole); anything off of the original

Broadway album from *The Wiz* or the movie *Waiting to Exhale* ("Shoop-Shoop," anyone?); and my favorite get-it-girl anthem, "You Gotta Be," by the UK's Des'ree.

Jammin' in the car, we'd trade grins in the rearview mirror as Veronica kicked in her car seat and I cranked the volume to amp our joy. Stevie, Luther, Chaka, Mariah, and plenty of TLC mixed it up with Sade, Whitney, Yolanda Adams, and my aunt, Sweetie, better known as Natalie Cole. I didn't inherit those incredible vocal chops, but whenever I sang, Veronica's dark eyes danced as if to say all the rest could come and go as long as she had me.

As I grew into motherhood, Veronica grew into her awareness and love of the music I fed her, and Beyoncé transformed from a shy girl who loved the stage to a budding powerhouse who had learned to command it. I observed her evolution from mere talent to force of nature with mild interest. Meanwhile, I marveled as my baby girl became her own person, with her own musical tastes, and a fan who would revere Beyoncé in a way that I have never revered anyone, to this day.

When *Dangerously in Love* dropped, Veronica was nine, the same age Beyoncé was when host Ed McMahon fumbled her name on *Star Search*. (Imagine not knowing how to say her name!)

To celebrate my firstborn's first double-digit birthday, I decided to give her something she would never forget, a night out at her first big concert.

The Madison Square Garden stop on the Verizon Ladies First Tour presented the perfect ticket at the perfect time. A triumvirate of A-list acts, it teamed Missy Elliott and Alicia

Keys with Beyoncé as the closer. "Special guest" Tamia was set to open the four-hour show.

It was a big deal, and not just because of the killer marquee. Never before had three top female R&B or hip hop acts (yup, that's Billboard code for Black) shared a single billing. In a comparison to the very successful, very white, all-female summer music festival of the late 1990s, the music press dubbed Ladies First the "urban Lilith Fair."

Veronica played piano and loved her some Alicia. Often, when she was supposed to be practicing, I would hear her from the living room, trying to peck out the notes to "Fallin'" or "If I Ain't Got You" instead. I was (and still am) a big Missy fan but, not sure I was ready to hear my fourth grader chirping "Get Ur Freak On," I kept most of Missy's hits on lock. For this one night, though, all that mattered was that Veronica was going to see Beyoncé, live!

To be honest, I had been torn about endorsing my deeply impressionable little girl's Beyoncéssion at first. Motherhood is rife with speed traps and music can be one of them. Granted, Bey was branded the sweetheart of hip hop, but "Bootylicious" was living in the same debatable time zone as most of Missy's music. And, with all due respect to hits like "Independent Women (Part 1)," those tight Destiny's Child costumes, stripper dance moves, and relationship-obsessed grooves hyped as "new feminism" felt like neither. Entertaining? Sure. Role models? Hmmm. The fact that the group struggled publicly with more than its share of infighting didn't help.

So, why did I eventually lay my misgivings aside and race to Target to buy Beyoncé's albums with the bonus tracks as soon as they dropped? My daughter loved the music (who didn't?). She saw herself in Bey, aspired to slay like Bey, and, a few iffy outfits aside, as idols went, Bey, like her many hits, was platinum.

Who worked harder? Dreamed bigger? Pushed herself further? Wanted, risked, and sacrificed more?

In her quest for independence, Beyoncé never once dishonored her parents or her roots. In her hunger for success, she displayed no appetite for haterade or competitive drama. (Her dad took the heat for Destiny's Child's discord while Bey deftly skirted any diva/mean-girl mess.) Drugs, booze, rehab? Nope, and any overt sexuality stayed squarely in the performance art lane. Crossing into adulthood, her tenaciousness seemed to bloom. However, even in her quest to own the future of music, Beyoncé regularly paid homage to its past, showing a reverence for her royal predecessors that clearly ran both ways.

At a Michael Jackson tribute concert two years after his death, Bey was introduced by none other than the King of Pop's three children. Before Bey, in a huge halo of an afro wig, launched into a mindblowing performance of the Jackson Five classic "I Wanna Be Where You Are," Paris Jackson earnestly proclaimed: "She carries the torch lit by our father."

After Tina Turner (aka the Queen of Rock) performed with Bey at the 2015 Grammys, she said she "felt proud" that Bey had "taken on the memory of my life in a really positive way." Even Prince (about whom Stevie Wonder once said, "If Michael Jackson was the King of Pop, Prince should be the Emperor") respected Bey enough to share a Grammy stage with her for a showstopping duet of "Purple Rain."

Asked which "young divas" she offered her blessing to in 2013, Natalie Cole called Beyoncé "the new Madonna. Girls want to look like her, they want to dress like her, she could be a great influence." Keenly aware that her great-niece, Veronica, was one of those girls, she added that Bey was "nice," and "definitely not a 'diva'" in the conventional sense.

Perhaps not, but Bey had grit. She took chances—unnecessary and very public risks—pushing the edges of her talents and skills hard even when doing so yielded mixed reviews (we nearly wore *The Fighting Temptations* DVD *out* in our house). She never played it safe, got defensive, or cowered from critics. She just got more coaching and took the next big chance.

Her perfectionism—such a common trap for girls and women—gave me pause. Yet, you could see that her zero tolerance for compromise was simply baked into her drive to be the best, and that it was as much about satisfying herself as anyone else. Ultimately, I decided, that made her a pretty damn good role model for my daughter or anyone, including me. So, I splurged on those Ladies First tickets, and we never looked back.

Bursting with anticipation on the drive to the Garden, Veronica grew tense as we made our way to our seats. The packed arena and her uncertainty about what to expect had made her watchful and quiet. Yet by the time Tamia, Missy, and Alicia finished their sets, Veronica was bathed in joy.

Sean "Puffy" Combs walked by, causing her to gawk and giggle, but then Beyoncé appeared and it was as if Puffy went poof.

There. She. Was. Reclined on a gilded platform that was being carried through the crowd by four shirtless, sculpted men. The lights bounced off of her scant 22-karat costume in tiny sparks as she tossed petals to her screaming fans. Shaheem Reid of MTV News gushed, "If Muhammad Ali had been at Madison Square Garden Monday night, no doubt he would've found something to pound like a drum as he yelled, 'The champ is here! The champ is here!' That's exactly the aura Beyoncé gave off as she began her closing set."

As Bey floated past us, Veronica followed with her entire body. Her big brown eyes grew wider, she sat up taller, rolled her narrow shoulders back, scooted to the edge of her seat, and leaned in, captivated, excited. Starstruck.

I was equally mesmerized, watching them both.

With her honey-spun mane flowing and the crowd's cheers colliding with the thumping intro to "Baby Boy," Beyoncé dismounted her regal perch, as if in slo-mo. But from the moment her metallic heels touched the stage, she took off—flinging hair, sequined hips, and rich, nimble vocals as if her life depended on it and she might never get another chance.

Several reviewers of previous shows had given the nod to Alicia as the standout, but Beyoncé was truly in her element at the Garden that night. Her soaring, searing vocals carried "Me, Myself and I" to unexpected heights, and when Jay-Z emerged for their duet on "Crazy in Love," there was no mistaking their killer chemistry, or the fact that we were witnessing real-time testimony when she sang, "You got me sprung and I don't care who sees 'cause, baby, you got me, you got me so crazy." (Me and V went crazy too; to this day, I defy anyone to be still when they hear that track.)

The crowd roared when Rowland and Williams appeared

for a medley of Destiny's Child hits, and when Bey, Kelly, and Michelle raised their fists for their defiant anthem, "Survivor," 20,000 fists went up with them. For a moment, the music stopped and there was just this powerful chant, echoing throughout the arena:

I'm a survivor
I'm gonna make it
I will survive
Keep on survivin'

Gazing at Veronica, her face serious, her skinny arm raised in the air like an upside-down exclamation point, my throat caught as I flashed back to my own mother and I, singing Aretha Franklin's "Respect" at the top of our lungs as we loaded the dishwasher and my father sat in the next room. It would be years before I realized that my mom sang when she was happy, and she sang when she was mad. "Respect" led her I'm-pissed hit parade, and she'd always belt it out within unmistakable earshot of my dad.

To this day, I never hear that song without thinking of my mother and her musical line in the sand. The posture she assumed whenever she sang it was one of defiance and determination, much like the one "Survivor" inspired in women of all ages decades later. As a child, I loved singing "Respect" with my mom (and Queen Aretha!) but I felt confused about what it meant and was too timid to ask. Gazing at Veronica chanting with her fist raised high, I smiled and saw history repeating itself. Survivor? She had no idea.

Captured in close-up on a giant screen above the stage, Beyoncé belted out the lyrics she helped write. The look on her face was not unlike my child's, pretending with all her might to be hard and grown and sure. I recognized her expression; in fact, I knew it well. Even in my thirties, a published author with a career, marriage, mortgage, and precious son to raise alongside my daughter, I sometimes wore it too. It's a mask that says, "I'm ready," even when you're not; even when you're doubtful, or hurting, or scared. Even when you're singing "R-E-S-P-E-C-T" at the top of your lungs, fooling your child into believing you're in a fun mood, when what you really want to do is cry.

Life seemed to spin out from that Ladies First moment, changing utterly and fast.

When Beyoncé upended the music industry *and the world* in 2016 by surprise-dropping her visual album, *Lemonade*, she was a 35-year-old artist, wife, and mother who had earned every one of those titles having survived quite a lot. She was also ready to share.

In full possession of herself, her vast influence, and compounding wealth, she did fewer interviews (a part of the business she never seemed to enjoy) and felt far less need for them. Crafting her own answers to her own questions and releasing them strategically, on her own terms, she masterfully manipulated the most valuable asset any of us has—her own narrative.

Documenting her evolution and projecting it through her own lens, that soft femininity that had endeared her to the press and her fans early on had become like her voice—riper, richer, stronger. Although journalists would still reference Sasha Fierce at times, Bey had no more need for alter egos. She showed up wherever she chose, as her fully integrated, complex, grown-and-unapologetic self. No longer hip hop's sweetheart, she had triumphed and endured enough to rightfully claim its throne ("Bow down, bitches!"), deploying every new media tool available to heighten the power that her talent, creativity, wealth, and, yes, choice of a husband had already earned her.

Veronica was 22 by then—the age B had been at that first solo concert—and she hadn't missed a tour since. Even when she had to mobilize her own network (and coins) to get there, Veronica was as front and center as she could manage—sometimes traveling to other states and occasionally catching the same show more than once. Her Aunt Sweetie was undone when she discovered that V had scored a better section at the Mrs. Carter show in Brooklyn than she did. When Natalie arrived at Barclays she scanned the upper tiers as she dialed Veronica, who promptly directed her to the middle of the floor where she stood on her tippy toes and waved until Natalie spotted her and fell out, laughing. Not only had V waited in line for hours to get onto the floor, she had been at the very same concert the night before.

As a gift for her college graduation, Veronica's Uncle Tommy gave her the best tickets she'd ever had, to the Formation World Tour at New York's Citi Field. As B and her stunning all-girl army stomped through *Freedom*, Veronica stood so close she could practically touch the stage. Her second score that night? She brought her reluctant brother, Carter, and finally converted him into a B-keeper too.

That show was a high point in a tough summer of transition.

By its end, Veronica would have moved out of our home, out of New York, and into her first real job and apartment. At times she felt mighty, at times scared and small. After a valiant battle with illness, Sweetie had died—too young—a few months before, and grief still hung heavily in the air. No matter what V was feeling, Bey had a song to help see her through.

I was there too, of course, but mothers and daughters don't always hear, see, or heed each other, and freedom isn't easy to cede or earn. Yet, as time passed, even when we were living in different states (or states of mind), I'd occasionally get a text or call out of nowhere, bursting with the latest news from the royal hive. Connecting over Beyoncé's journey had become a part of our own.

Perhaps when Beyoncé thinks back on the Ladies First Tour, she views it as a shimmering time when life was simple, even as she made her own first bold, life-altering moves. She was already a star. For most, that would have been enough. But Bey stays hungry; you can still see it in her eyes. Veronica now has that look too.

I continue to observe them both as I did that night, filled with a mix of anxiety and awe, wondering what they'll do next, how they'll use their voices, and what they may have to survive to make their dreams come true. Life is not easy for women of power and for those of color it is harder still, even in a world overflowing with followers and fans. So I cheer and pray for us all, but especially for Veronica, as I watch, smiling, from the edge of my seat, my Queen Bey playlist on blast for the ride, captivated, excited. Starstruck.

About the Contributors

———◆———

VERONICA CHAMBERS is a prolific writer and the author of the critically acclaimed memoir *Mama's Girl* and the editor of the bestselling *The Meaning of Michelle*, a *Time* Non-Fiction Top Ten of the Year. She is currently editor of archival storytelling at the *New York Times*. A JSK Fellow at Stanford in 2017, she's been a senior editor at the *New York Times Magazine*, *Glamour*, and *Newsweek*. Follow her on Twitter and Instagram @vvchambers and online at Veronicachambers.com.

LUVVIE AJAYI is a Nigerian author, speaker, and digital strategist. Her first book, *I'm Judging You: The Do-Better Manual*, was a *New York Times* bestseller. Ajayi began her career in marketing and digital strategy and started blogging in 2003. Her site AwesomelyLuvvie.com amassed a following, particularly for Ajayi's recaps of television shows like *Scandal*, drawing the attention of *Scandal* showrunner Shonda Rhimes. In 2016, *The New York Times* reported that Ajayi had an audience of approximately

500,000 between her personal Twitter feed and the Awesomely Luvvie website. In 2016, Ajayi was the first writer invited to speak at the National Museum of African American History and Culture, and her event sold out.

LENA WAITHE is an actor, producer, and screenwriter. She has starred in *Master of None* and *The Chi*, and was the first Black woman to win an Emmy for writing comedy for her work on *Master of None*. She produced *Dear White People, Step Sisters,* and starred in *Ready Player One*.

BRITTNEY COOPER is the author of *Eloquent Rage*. A professor of Women's and Gender Studies and Africana Studies at Rutgers University, she co-founded the Crunk Feminist Collective, and her work has appeared in *The New York Times, The Washington Post,* Ebony.com, and theroot.com, among many other places. In 2018, she was named to *The Root* 100 List and to the *Essence* Woke 100 List.

KID FURY is a YouTube vlogger, comedian, and co-host of podcast *The Read*, with Crissle West. He won the Shorty Award for YouTuber of the Year in 2014.

YLONDA GAULT is the author of the parenting memoir *Child, Please* and a *New York Times* op-ed contributor. An award-winning journalist, she has specialized in issues related to child advocacy, family, and motherhood for more than a decade. Gault's work has appeared in *Essence, The New York Times, Redbook,* and Salon.com. She is a single mom of three awesome children.

MARIA BRITO is an award-winning New York–based contemporary art advisor, creative designer, author, and curator. A Harvard grad, originally from Venezuela, Maria has worked with Sean "Diddy" Combs and Gwyneth Paltrow and has built the art collections of prominent CEOs, entrepreneurs, and fashion executives, sharing her knowledge and creativity with them to turn her clients into meaningful art collectors. Her first book *Out There* was the recipient of two USA Best Book Awards in the Art and Design categories. Maria and her projects have been featured extensively in national and international publications, including *The New York Times Style Section, T: The New York Times Magazine, The Wall Street Journal, Huffington Post, W* magazine, *ELLE Magazine,* and *Harper's BAZAAR.*

MELISSA HARRIS-PERRY is the Maya Angelou Presidential Chair at Wake Forest University. There she is founding director of the Anna Julia Cooper Center. The AJC Center's mission is to advance justice through intersectional scholarship. Harris-Perry is editor-at-large at Elle.com and a nationally recognized scholar and teacher. She is author of the award-winning *Barbershops, Bibles, and BET: Everyday Talk and Black Political Thought,* and *Sister Citizen: Shame, Stereotypes, and Black Women in America.* Her innovative teaching has been recognized and replicated by colleagues throughout the country. In 2016, Professor Harris-Perry founded and co-directed the innovative, bipartisan, student democratic engagement program Wake the Vote.

MANKAPRR CONTEH is a writer and multimedia journalist exploring music, identity, and social issues. She has written and reported for Elle.com, Essence.com, Okayplayer, and other outlets, and has worked on radio and podcasts at 88.5 WFDD in North Carolina and WNYC Studios in New York.

MEREDITH BROUSSARD is an assistant professor at the Arthur L. Carter Journalism Institute of New York University and the author of *Artificial Unintelligence: How Computers Misunderstand the World.* Her current research focuses on artificial intelligence in investigative reporting, with a particular interest in using data analysis for social good. A former features editor at *The Philadelphia Inquirer,* she has also worked as a software developer at AT&T Bell Labs and the MIT Media Lab. Her features and essays have appeared in *The Atlantic, Harper's,* Slate .com, and other outlets. Follow her on Twitter @merbroussard or contact her via meredithbroussard.com.

ELODIE MAILLIET STORM manages Getty Images' relationships with more than 300 editorial and creative content partners around the world, including *National Geographic, Sky News, Bloomberg,* and *Condé Nast.* Storm also launched Getty Images' high-end portraiture and fashion division, Contour, which she led until 2014. Before joining Getty, she was director of photography for portraiture and entertainment at Corbis. Storm is on the board of the Emmy award–winning multimedia documentary production company MediaStorm. In 2005, she was named one of the top 11 people in photography by *American Photo.* Storm has worked as a freelance writer for *Le Nouvel Observateur, VSD,* and French *Photo.*

MICHAEL ERIC DYSON is one of America's premier public intellectuals and the author of the instant *New York Times* bestseller *Tears We Cannot Stop.* He occupies the distinguished position of University Professor of Sociology at Georgetown University, is a contributing opinion writer for *The New York Times,* and is a contributing editor of *The New Republic* and ESPN's *The Undefeated. Ebony* magazine named him one of the 100 Most Influential African Americans and one of the 150 most powerful blacks in the nation.

RESHMA SAUJANI is the founder of Girls Who Code. She began her career as an attorney and activist. In 2010, she surged onto the political scene as the first Indian American woman to run for U.S. Congress. During the race, Reshma visited local schools and saw the gender gap in computing classes firsthand, which led her to start Girls Who Code. Reshma has also served as deputy public advocate for New York City and ran a spirited campaign for public advocate in 2013.

CANDICE BENBOW is a writer and a creative. Through writing, Candice's essays give voice to the shared experiences of heartbreak, grief, and the journey toward wholeness and life. Following the release of Jay-Z's thirteenth studio album, *4:44,* Candice wrote "4:43," chronicling the stories of women who are caught on the underside of the growth of men. It has been read over 300,000 times and over 100,000 times across social media platforms. In addition to her own blog, her work has appeared in *Glamour, Essence, Ebony,* The Root, Urban Cusp, *Religion & Politics,* For Harriet, and Patheos.

CARMEN PEREZ is the executive director of The Gathering for Justice, a nonprofit founded by Harry Belafonte, and has crossed the globe promoting peace through civil and human rights, building alternatives to incarceration and violence, and providing commentary and guidance for state and federal policy creation. Her work inside of juvenile detention centers and prisons in California and New York has provided cultural, spiritual, and educational events as well as individual support to incarcerated youth. Carmen is the co-founder of Justice League NYC and founder of Justice League CA, two state-based task forces for advancing the juvenile and criminal justice reform agenda. She has organized numerous national convenings, including Growing Up Locked Down conferences on juvenile justice, and the March2Justice, a 250-mile march that drew congressional attention to key legislative reforms to confront the national crisis in police violence. A respected expert in the field of juvenile and criminal justice and system accountability, Carmen was invited to testify before the President's Task Force on 21st Century Policing and has been featured in numerous media outlets.

ISABEL GONZÁLEZ WHITAKER is a Presidential Leadership Scholar who established the first Hispanic memorial park in Georgia, the Sara J. Gonzalez Park. She was previously a features editor at *InStyle* and deputy editor of *Billboard*.

EDWARD ENNINFUL is editor in chief of British *Vogue*. Enninful joined the title after a six-year stint as style director of *W* magazine. The Ghanaian-born stylist began his career as fashion director of British youth culture magazine *i-D* at age 18, the youngest ever to have been named an editor at a major international fashion title. After moving to London with his parents and six siblings at a young age, Enninful was scouted as a model on the train at 16 and briefly modeled for *Arena* and *i-D* magazines before assisting stylists Simon Foxton and Beth Summers on fashion shoots. His fashion stories, often infused with a provocative elegance and strong narrative, have also appeared in American *Vogue* and *Vogue Italia*, where he was a contributing editor. In 2011, Enninful was tapped to take the style directorship at *W* magazine.

FATIMA ROBINSON was named one of *Entertainment Weekly*'s "100 most creative people in Entertainment." Renowned for her ability to blend classic dance styles with her distinct hip hop flavor, Fatima has choreographed for notable spots including Target, Chanel, H&M, Burberry, Pepsi, Gap, iPod, Nissan, Verizon, Motorola, and Heineken. Fatima has worked with Britney Spears, Meghan Trainor, Pharrell Williams, Black Eyed Peas, Fergie, Gwen Stefani, Lana Del Rey, Usher, Sade, Prince, Rihanna, Major Lazer, Kendrick Lamar, and Mary J. Blige. Fatima choreographed NBC's live television production of *The Wiz*, which aired last holiday season. She also served as segment producer for the Weeknd's performance of "Earned It" at the 2015 Academy Awards, and choreographed Pharrell's unforgettable performance of the hit song "Happy" at the 2014 Academy Awards. She also notably choreographed the 2011 Super Bowl Halftime Show with the Black Eyed Peas, the 2012 Coachella Tupac hologram, as well as the 2007 and 2009 Academy Awards, making her the second African American woman in history to do so.

EBRO DARDEN is a media executive and radio presenter. Until 2014, Darden was vice president of programming for Emmis Communications' New York contemporary urban station WQHT (Hot 97). He is currently a co-host on the Hot 97 morning show *Ebro in the Morning*, alongside Peter Rosenberg and Laura Stylez. Darden also hosts a hip hop music–based radio show on Beats 1.

TREVA B. LINDSEY is associate professor of African American women's history, Black popular and expressive culture, Black feminism(s), hip hop studies, critical race and gender theory, and sexual politics at Ohio State University.

ROBIN M. BOYLORN is associate professor of interpersonal and intercultural communication at the University of Alabama, where she teaches and writes about issues of social identity and diversity, focusing primarily on the lived experience(s) of Black women. She is the author of *Sweetwater: Black Women and Narratives of Resilience*, co-writer (with Brittney C. Cooper and Susana M. Morris) of *The Crunk Feminist Collection*, and co-editor of *Critical Autoethnography: Intersecting Cultural Identities in Everyday Life*. Her writing has appeared in Slate.com, *Ebony*, Salon.com, *The Guardian*, Gawker.com, and The Crunk Feminist Collective.

CAROLINE CLARKE is an award-winning journalist and author whose experience spans print, digital, and television. At Black Enterprise, she has served in a number of key roles including general manager, Interactive Media; editor at large, *Black Enterprise* magazine; and editorial director, Black Enterprise Books. She is currently host of the *Women of Power* TV show and editorial director of the Women of Power Summit. Drawing more than 1,000 registrants each year and a host of blue-chip sponsors, the summit is the nation's largest annual conference targeting women-of-color executives.

Acknowledgments

———•———

I compiled this collection with the help of my amazing editor, Elisabeth Dyssegaard. There's a phrase in Spanish—*sin palabras*—which means words don't suffice. That's how I feel about Elisabeth. Isabel Gonzalez Whitaker acted as a managing editor for a project with a lot of moving parts. I'm grateful to both Elisabeth and Isabel for their vision, energy, and enthusiasm. I first met the St. Martin's team when we worked on a collection about our forever First Lady, *The Meaning of Michelle*. Thank you to Alan Bradshaw, Staci Burt, and Laura Apperson for editorial guidance and heroic patience. Thanks to copy editors for careful reading: Jennifer Simington, Rima Weinberg, Lisa Davis.

The character Michael has a hilarious line on the TV show *The Good Place*. He says, "Any place or thing in the universe can be up to 104 percent perfect. That's how you got Beyoncé." Anthologies are all about the mix, and to me, this group of writers is 104 percent perfect. Thank you to: Luvvie Ajayi, Candice Benbow, Maria Brito, Robin M. Boylorn, Meredith Broussard, Brittney Cooper, Ebro Darden, Sir Edward Enninful,

Kid Fury, Ylonda Gault, Isabel González Whitaker, Melissa Harris-Perry and Mankaprr Conteh, Treva B. Lindsey, Elodie Mailliet Storm, Carmen Perez, Fatima Robinson, Reshma Saujani, and Lena Waithe. Michael Eric Dyson inspires me with the way he leads, teaches, and creates—both on and off the page. I'm so honored to have his voice in this book. We loved the visualizations by Andrew Harvard and Juan Carlos Mora. A special thanks to Caroline Clarke for both her essay in this book and for all the offline conversations and cheerleading that kept me going. Samantha Shankman and Rachel Bowie are great second readers for me. Jason Clampet is my IR—my ideal reader—and I'm lucky to have him as my first editor and life partner.

I'm thankful that my daughter, Flora, gets to grow up in the Black girl magic universe that Beyoncé helped build and to Beyoncé herself, for showing us time and time again all the ways in which we are limitless.